# LABRADOR RETRIEVER

Esther Verhoef

# LABRADOR RETRIEVER

REBO PUBLISHERS

Text: Esther Verhoef
Photographs: Esther Verhoef
Cover design and layout: Mesika Design, Hilversum, The Netherlands
Typesetting and pre-press services: AdAm Studio, Prague, The Czech Republic
Americanization: Andrew Mikolajski for First Edition Translations Ltd, Cambridge, UK
Proofreading: Sarah Dunham

ISBN 13: 978-90-366-1561-7
ISBN 10: 90-366-1561-5

# TABLE OF CONTENTS

# 1 HISTORY

## Newfoundland

The Labrador Retriever originated in the North America. In the eighteenth century, the fishermen on the island of Newfoundland had two types of dog to help them with their work. One type was a large, black dog with a thick coat which we now know as the Newfoundland, the other was a smaller dog of lighter build and with shorter hair, the predecessor of the Labrador Retriever. The fishermen had many trade contacts with England, and exchanged their working dogs as well as their wares. This is how the dogs of Newfoundland originally came to England, where the more lightly-built dog aroused the interest of the English upper classes. Until 1814, both types of dog were called "Newfoundlands," until the smaller type was ultimately named "St. John's Dog" or "Labrador."

*Labradors from around the turn of the century*

## From fisherman's dog to gun dog

*Right: The Labrador Retriever was originally a hunting dog*

Although Labrador Retrievers on Newfoundland served mainly as fishermen's helpers – among other things, they helped to pull in the nets – the English nobility discovered that the breed had all the qualities to function well on the hunting

grounds. To improve the working capacity, every now and then they were cross-bred with other breeds, such as the Pointer, but also with Setters, Spaniels, and Flatcoated Retrievers. Although these animals were far from purebred, they were still allowed to be shown and even won championships. A number of fanciers were not happy with this situation and formed the English Labrador Retriever Club, which set the breed standard and also had the objective of keeping the breed as pure as possible.

The Labrador Reriever was officially recognized as a purebred dog by the English Kennel Club in 1903.

## The colors

From the beginning, most Labrador Retrievers have had a black coat. Yellow did occur, but it was not the color preferred by hunters. The first registered yellow Labrador Retriever, named Ben of Hyde, was born in 1889; nevertheless, it took another ten years before the color was accepted in hunters' circles. The now so popular chocolate-colored coat is of a more recent date. It was first described in 1938.

***Three colors of Labrador***

## Banchory Bolo

One of the most well-known and also most remarkable Labradors of the early period was the black Labrador Retriever dog Banchory Bolo, born in England in 1915. With his equally well-known owner, Lorna, Countess Howe, Bolo was the first Labrador Retriever to win the beauty as well as the working championship. Bolo had unique, white spots at the rear of the soles of his paws. Every now and then, puppies are still born with the same unique trait. They are then said to have "Bolo pads" and are direct descendants of this Labrador Retriever, one of the very first.

# 2 Breed Standard

## Head

The Labrador Retriever has a broad skull with a clear stop. The head is sharply outlined, without fleshy cheeks. The jaws are moderately long, powerful, and do not taper to a point. The nose is broad with well-developed nostrils. The ears are not large or heavy, lie close to the head, and are set relatively far back. The eyes are medium large, with an intelligent and friendly expression. They are brown or hazel-colored. The jaws are strong. The Labrador Retriever has a perfect, regular, and completely scissored

*The Labrador has a broad skull with a clear stop*

bite; the upper teeth fall exactly over the lower teeth and stand straight in the jaw.

## Body

*Right: Two different tones of brown*

The neck is dry, strong, and sturdy, and placed on well-set shoulders. The shoulders are long and sloping. The breast is suffi-

ciently wide and deep, with well-arched ribs. The loins are broad, short, and strong. Well-developed hindquarters, not sloping toward the tail. The forelegs have sturdy bones. Seen from both the front and the side, they stand straight from the elbow to the ground. The hind legs have a well-angled knee and low-placed heels. Cow heels are absolutely not desired. The paws are round and compact, with well-arched toes and well-developed soles. The tail is typical of the breed. It is very thick at the base, tapering to a point, of medium length, free of feathering, but covered all around with a short, thick coat. This gives it a round shape, described as an "otter's tail." It should be carried gaily, but should not curl over the back.

## Shoulder height

Males have a shoulder height between 22.5 in. and 23 in. (56 cm and 57 cm); for bitches, this is 21.5 in. and 22.5 in. (54 cm to 56 cm).

## Coat

The coat is typical of the breed. It feels fairly hard and is short and dense, without waves or feathering. The undercoat is weather-resistant.

*There are different shades of yellow*

## Color

Labrador Retrievers are found in the colors yellow, black, or liver/chocolate. The yellow color can vary from light cream to fox red. A small, white spot on the breast is permitted.

## Temperament

Intelligent, lively, and obedient, with a strong will to please the owner. Friendly character without a trace of aggression or inappropriate shyness.

*Black Labrador Retriever male*

# 3 Character and Possibilities for Use

## Gun dogs

The Labrador Retriever has always been a gun dog, speciali-zed in one aspect of the hunt: finding and bringing shot game to the hunter. The dog has several characteristics that enable it to do this work properly. A good retriever will always hold the game very gently, so that it is damaged as little as possible. Insiders call this "gentle in the mouth," and, translated into

*Labradors are excellent retrievers*

*Right: Tired but satisfied after a hard day's work*

ROYAL CANIN

a family situation, this means that a Labrador is not a biter by nature and accepts the objects and treats offered carefully. A good Retriever must not frighten easily and must remain stable and calm when it hears sudden loud noises. A dog that shrinks with fear or runs away with its tail between its legs when it hears gunshot is not a good gun dog. Many Labradors do make good gun dogs; a loud noise or whatever kind of commotion will seldom or never result in panic. Another quality that a good Retriever has by nature is that it likes to obey. It should not go running or barking after game on its own, or be a nuisance in any other way. Finally, its endurance must be excellent and it should not be afraid of diving into (cold) water.

## Working dogs

In addition to being gun dogs, Labradors are also used for other work. They are known as guide dogs for the blind, but are also especially good assistants for invalids. They can open doors, turn lights on and off, and do many other daily tasks that the dog's owner can only do with difficulty or not at all. Labrador Retrievers also function as warning dogs. During their training, such dogs learn to warn their deaf or hard-of-hearing owner of sounds, such as the front doorbell.

We also see Labrador Retrievers working as rescue dogs, where the emphasis is on searching for people. An outstanding sense of smell and a drive to work are essential for a rescue dog. The same qualities are needed by Labrador Retrievers that are used

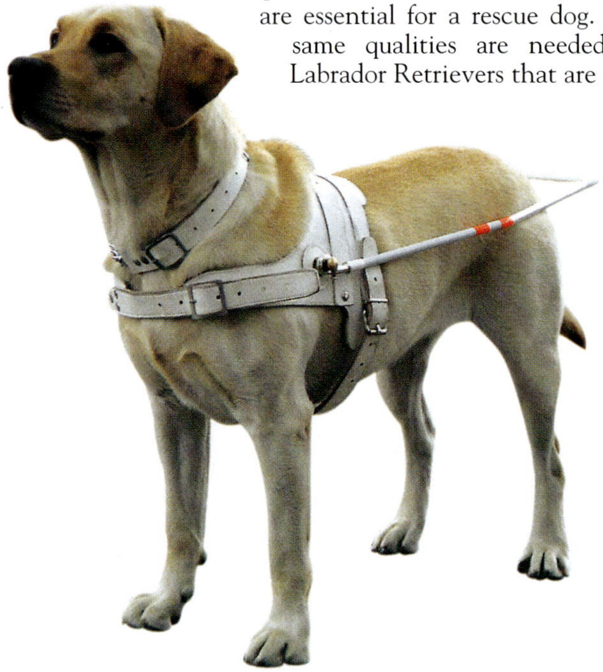

***This young bitch is being trained as a guide dog for the blind***

to detect explosives and drugs. At many borders and at virtually every international airport and many international seaports, we find Labrador Retrievers doing this important work on a daily basis. Although many Labrador Retrievers possess many of these qualities, such as the will to work, a good nose, and optimum obedience, this does not mean that all dogs of this breed are suitable for these functions. Many institutes that train guide dogs for the blind breed their own future guide dogs and select the older animals as well as the puppies for the desired qualities. Nor is every Labrador Retriever suitable for other disciplines. A lot depends on the (inherited) will to work of the parents and ancestors, and the dogs must undergo long and thorough training before they can be deployed.

## The Labrador Retriever as a family dog

Although the number of working dogs cannot be underestimated, the vast majority of these dogs are kept exclusively as companions. Labradors are eminently suitable for this, but it

***A Labrador loves retrieving and being outdoors***

*A Labrador does not like to be shut out of the house*

is a pity that so many people neglect the many qualities of their dog. A Labrador Retriever likes to have something to do. It will not become bothersome if it is not given any tasks, but will lose much pleasure in life if it has to spend its days in front of the fireplace. The dog enjoys accompanying you on long walks, never tires of retrieving balls, and likes to obey commands. Most of all, however, a Labrador wants to be with the family and take part in everyday life. It is not a one-person dog, nor is it shy.

## Not a watchdog

Although the Labrador Retriever is by nature a very social gun dog who always greets your visitors in a friendly manner, it will bark if it finds that things are not as they should be. This breed cannot be called a true defender of house, home, and family, nor is the Labrador Retriever intended for this, but, when the need arises, your Labrador Retriever will not let you down.

## Labradors and children

It is in the nature of most Labradors to get along well with children. Loud noises, screaming and running children, and all other factors that would be a source of stress for other dogs, have little or no effect on a well-socialized Labrador Retriever. The dog usually reacts gently and calmly to this. Nevertheless, you should realize that Labrador Retrievers, especially the males, are big, strong dogs. When young, they are exuberant and active, indoors as well as outside. In their youthful enthusiasm, they could easily knock over a small child. If you have very young children, you will have to watch out for this.

## The Labrador and other animals

A well-socialized and well-bred Labrador Retriever can live together with other pets, be it a cat or horse, without any problem. Because of their background as gun dogs, they usually have a more than average interest in animals such as chickens and rabbits. They must learn while very young that they should not hunt these animals. Labrador Retrievers are uncomplicated dogs, who usually get along very well with

***Labradors are always ready to play***

*This dog always wants to please its owner*

other dogs. Amongst themselves, there are seldom problems of rank, and they have no tendency to challenge other dogs on the street, although this depends to a great extent on the characters of the parent animals and the manner in which the dog has been raised and socialized.

## Will to please

Labradors are known for their will to please. This is expressed, among other ways, in an obedient and kind attitude toward their owner and the other family members. Most Labradors are fast learners-since a Labrador, despite all its positive qualities, naturally is and remains a dog with dog-like qualities. The Labrador Retriever, too, can have a bad day and be contrary. Contrary reactions can be expected especially around puberty. Disobedience, however, can only result from too monotonous training, a physical disorder, and poor, too hard, or inconsistent raising. It is not true that your Labrador Retriever puppy will automatically understand what you tell it. All this has to be taught and, even though the dog learns quickly, raising and training it will definitely require your time and insight. If you choose a dog of this breed because you think that not much raising or training is necessary, you will certainly be disappointed.

## Water

The predisposition for water is an inborn characteristic of almost every Labrador. It is not easy for them to walk calmly by a lake or dirty mud puddle. This causes practical problems if you are fond of a tidy house or a clean car. It is, of course, not the intention to allow your dog to swim or roll

***Mad about water***

about in mud puddles whenever it wants. If given the chance, this will occur several times during every walk. See to it that your Labrador Retriever listens well to commands, so that you can call it back if its intentions do not correspond with yours.

## The young Labrador Retriever

However careful, obedient, and wise an adult Labrador may be, as a young dog it can be as boisterous, exuberant, naughty, and impulsive as any other pup. Many Labrador puppies resemble miniature bulldozers that see your house as one, big playground. No mud puddle remains unwallowed in and, exuberant as they are, they do not take any account of the fragility of the objects they might collide with in their path of destruction. Puppies like to test the strength of their sharp teeth, and Labradors in puberty often simply "forget" that they are only supposed to chew their own toys and safety bones. Puberty begins rather early in Labradors, sometimes even from four months, although the replacement of their milk teeth also plays a part in their increased need

*Can you imagine this in your backyard.... You think it's fun? Very good*

to chew. This period is usually over by the first birthday. Nevertheless, the adult Labrador is still an enthusiastic dog that often wags its strong tail, which can easily knock the cups off the coffee table. You should understand that keeping a Labrador Retriever cannot always be combined with a tidy house and clean clothes. Therefore, consider carefully beforehand whether you would be able to accept such spontaneous behavior in your dog and also appreciate the fun of them.

*Retrieving, at any time, is great fun for a Labrador*

*Far right: Beautiful black Labrador Retriever bitch*

# 4 ACQUISITION

## Considerations in advance

Your Labrador Retriever can live for ten years or more and is completely dependent on you every day for exercise, feeding, and care. Throughout the dog's life, you will be responsible for its well-being, and not one day will pass without the dog having an influence on the daily course of life in the family. Having a dog does not only involve the pleasant aspects, but also the less pleasant ones, which you must consider carefully before taking such an adorable puppy into your home.
If you go on holiday and are unable to take the dog along, you will have to find good boarding kennels or a reliable dog-sitter. This must be done in good time, because in the summer periods good kennels are often fully booked months in advance. Although the coat of a Labrador does not need a lot of grooming, a dog in the house always means more housework. You will have to vacuum more often and, because of its love of water, the mop and pail will be in use on a regular basis.
If you have a dog, of whatever breed, this also means that you must fight the battle with worms and fleas, and that you must take your dog to the veterinary surgeon at least once a year for the requisite vaccinations. It may be that you only see your veterinary surgeon once a year, but it is also possible that your dog will get sick and need veterinary assistance. Costs can escalate. Labrador Retrievers are large dogs with a heal-

*A half-grown dog can be a good choice*

thy appetite. The purchase price of a Labrador Retriever is only a fraction of what the dog will cost throughout its life. Ask yourself honestly if you have the time and money for this, and if you will be able to provide your dog with what it needs for the coming ten years or more, day after day.

## Male or female?

The choice of a male or a female is personal. The biggest difference between males and females is their strength and size. Males are larger and stronger than females and therefore need an owner who is literally sturdy on his or her own feet. Another difference between the sexes is that females only urinate when necessary and in a squatting position, while adult males not only urinate when they feel the urge, but also do it to mark their territory. If you have a tidy garden to which you have devoted much time and effort, you will have to consider this as well.
The bitch's estrous cycles is an obstacle for some people. She must be watched carefully twice a year during the entire heat, which lasts approximately three weeks. If you think that you will not be able to do this, you can have a periodic anti-heat shot administered or have her spayed (uterus removed).

## Puppy or half-grown/fully grown dog?

If prizes were given for puppies with the most endearing and pettable appearance, Labrador Retrievers would undoubted-

*Males are stronger and larger than females*

*A ten-week old chocolate puppy*

ly be among the top five. It is no surprise that most people choose a Labrador puppy. Not only the dog's appearance, but the fact that it can be raised in accordance with their own ideas, are the reasons most people want to have this breed of pup. Every now and again, half or fully grown dogs are offered. These may be breeding bitches or stud dogs which do not pass on the desired qualities to their descendants, but also dogs in need of a new home for whatever reason. There is every reason to choose an older dog if it has been given a good grounding elsewhere. Older dogs generally adjust very well to new circumstances and become as attached to their new family as a young pup would. Older dogs are usually house-trained, have their pubescent mischief behind them, and know the most important commands. If you dread upbringing and house-training, an older dog is a good choice. Make thorough inquiries about its previous history. Be wary if the dog appears to have a disease or defect, or perhaps has annoying character traits which are difficult to live with. These dogs may ultimately function very well but will, of course, require much attention as well as the services of an expert veterinary surgeon or behavioral retraining.

## The first one you happen to find?

Labradors have been among the top five most popular breeds of dog for many years. The great demand for Labrador Retrievers attracts "breeders" who wish to profit financially from such popularity. These people are not really interested in the health and well-being of the puppies and their parents and ancestors, but only in the proceeds of their "breeding farms." You may have good luck at such an address, but the chance is great that you will return home with a puppy that ultimately fails to meet your expectations on one or more points or even has a defect or disease.

*Yellow male*

*Good gun dogs often have parents and ancestors that were selected for good hunting qualities*

Several hereditary defects are known to occur in this breed. Hip and elbow dysplasia and eye defects are a source of concern and attention for serious breeders, who have their prospective breeding dogs tested for this type of problem. Therefore, not every address where puppies are offered is reliable. To be sure that the puppy you acquire is genetically predisposed to grow into a healthy dog with a stable character and the characteristic appearance of the breed, you would be well advised to contact the puppy intermediary section of the Labrador Club. They will be able to supply you with addresses or telephone numbers of breeders who do things properly and can be expected to breed healthy, stable dogs. The address is listed at the back of this book.

## Different bloodlines

Perhaps you want a Labrador Retriever because you are looking for a good family dog, but it could also be, for example, that at some point in the future a litter, visits to a show,

*They all look alike, but there is a difference*

or training for the hunt might be desirable. If you set such requirements on your future housemate, it goes without saying that you must also set greater store by its pedigree. Character traits are partly hereditary, which also applies to appearance and certain disciplines. The chance of finding a good gun dog in a litter of which the parents and grandparents had proven themselves in the field is many times greater than if you simply choose a puppy from a litter for which the parents and ancestors were mainly selected for their

*By handling puppies regularly, you accustom them to contact with people*

attractive appearance, and vice versa. Of course, there are a large number of breeders who pay attention both to appearance and working qualities. Even if these qualities are not mutually exclusive, it is wise in such a case to seek information from the breed club.

## Imprinting

A very important phase in a dog's life, the imprinting phase, runs from the third up to about the seventh week of life. The puppy spends this phase of life with the breeder. During the imprinting phase, a puppy becomes aware for the first time of the world around it. It hears sounds, for example from the television and vacuum cleaner, sees and hears children playing, and is picked up and cuddled. Pups born indoors, in the living room or kitchen, do not need additional imprinting. These puppies become acquainted with the world on a daily basis, and take all that noise for granted. However, if the puppies grow up in an isolated place, it is the breeder's task to ensure that they are in contact with everyday things at least fifteen minutes a day. If this is not done, there is a good chance that the puppies will grow into fearful, apathetic, and maladjusted dogs that are unable to function in any family. Behavioral problems resulting from incorrect imprinting are permanent. A good breeder knows this and takes the responsibility seriously. The risk of bad imprinting occurs primarily with the so-called "backyard" breeders.

## What must you watch out for?

Good wine praises itself, and that certainly applies to puppies. A breeder who breeds good dogs is more interested in whether you can provide a good home for the puppy than in the financial gain received. Take a good look at how the dogs

react to the breeder. You can tell a lot from this. Examine the hygiene in the litter and its surroundings.

***Puppies' behavior reveals a lot about their character and living conditions***

For imprinting, it is best for the puppies to be raised in the vicinity of people. Observe the bitch. You are a stranger to her and she feels responsible for the safety of her puppies, so she may well be a bit reserved. It is different if she is too mistrustful, anxious, or even reacts aggressively. An unstable character can be hereditary but, even if her nervous condition does not have a hereditary basis, she is not a good example for her puppies. Also pay attention to the behavior of the puppies them-

***Chocolate-brown older lady***

*Two bitches of different colors*

selves. Healthy puppies are enterprising and playful. If they are not too sleepy, they will come and make your acquaintance. Pups that react to you with disinterest, shyness, or apathy can better be left where they are. A too fat stomach, motley coat, traces of diarrhea, and runny eyes and nose are not good signs. The sire of the litter may be present, but this is not necessary. Many breeders use the services of a "foreign" male, so that you can only see photos of him there. Ask in any case to see the results of tests for hip and elbow dysplasia for the sire as well as the dam, and study them well to avoid acquiring puppies with a (partly) hereditary defect. These defects cannot be tested at a very early age, so it is important that the parent animals, and preferably their parents as well, have been officially declared free.

## The choice

*A healthy, happy, and playful group of puppies*

It may be that the puppies have not yet been vaccinated. In such a case, the breeder may not want you to touch or come too close to them. You could unwittingly have taken in germs and be a potential source of infection to the pups. The breeder does not know you and cannot know whether you have visited other breeders earlier that day, with less hygienic conditions. If the puppies have been completely immunized,

these objections will naturally not apply and you can go among the pups to make your choice.

A persistent fairy tale is that you must choose the puppy that first comes to you. Healthy, open, and well-imprinted puppies will all come to you. The first one that dares is often the freshest of the bunch and will usually grow into a dominant dog that would be better off with a more dominant owner with special insight into bringing up a dog. If these characteristics apply to you, you can safely choose such a puppy. There is often one puppy in the litter that is more cautious and approaches you more carefully than the others. Such a puppy would not do well in a bustling, busy family with children. It would be better for this puppy to be taken into quiet surroundings, with calm people who have the time and patience to help such a shy dog gain more self-confidence and provide a stable upbringing. If you find it difficult to make a

*A slender Labrador like this one is not considered a good show dog*

choice, ask the breeder for an opinion. The breeder is with the puppies every day and knows them better than anyone else. Taking the family situation and future plans as described by you as a guideline, the breeder is the best one to tell you which of the puppies in the litter would be most suitable for your circumstances.

## Papers

If your puppy has been vaccinated, tattooed, and/or chipped, you can often take it along immediately. If this has not yet been done, you will have to be patient for a while. Puppies are tattooed at the age of six to nine weeks or receive a subcutaneous identification chip, and at about eight to ten weeks they are old enough to go to their new homes.
Ask the breeder for a rag with the scent of the litter. At home, this rag can be placed in the basket or crate, so that the pup will feel somewhat more at ease. The breeder cannot yet give you a pedigree, because the administration of this takes some time. This will be brought or sent to you later. If you have acquired your dog from an address unknown to the breed club, you must make sure that your dog has been chipped or tat-

tooed when you get it. If this is not the case, your dog will have no right to a pedigree.

In addition to a rag with the scent of the litter, the breeder will give you the immunization booklet, a health certificate, and a feeding schedule. The immunization booklet contains a list of when, against what, and with what medicine your dog has been vaccinated, and when the booster shots are due. A health certificate is issued by the breeder's veterinary surgeon, in which it is certified that at the time the puppy was examined, it was healthy with no visible defects. A feeding schedule contains information on the quantities and sorts of food your pup is accustomed to and at what times you can best feed it.

*Breeders and their dogs can also be found at shows*

More and more breeders also work with contracts of sale, in which the rights and obligations of both the buyer and the seller are laid down and which must be signed by both parties. Check whether the contents of the contract of sale are reasonable before signing it.

# 5 YOUR PUPPY AT HOME

## Going home

Your new housemate can best be picked up by car, together with someone else, so that one can drive and the other can mind the puppy. If the trip is long, you must stop on the way to give your puppy the chance to relieve itself, to drink, and (on the leash!) to stretch its legs. Some pupppies get carsick and throw up, but if the breeder has not fed the puppy beforehand you should not expect any problems.

*Promising young black male*

Once home, you can give the dog one more chance to relieve itself before taking it inside. In most cases, the puppy has only had a preliminary immunization, which means that it is not yet sufficiently protected against several dangerous, contagious diseases. To prevent your dog from getting infected and falling sick, during the first few weeks you should only let it out in your own garden or take it to places where few or preferably no other dogs go.

## At home

During the first few hours, let the puppy sniff a bit around the house. Do not follow it, do not call it, and tell your children to leave it alone. Your puppy has too many new impressions to deal with. Place the rag from the litter in its basket or crate, so that your puppy knows that this will be its sleeping place from now on. Teach your children to leave their sleeping housemate alone. Your puppy's sleeping place is its domain, where it must be able to isolate itself if tired or wanting to sleep.

*Right: During the trip home someone can hold the puppy on his or her lap*

Teach your children that they must never pick up the puppy. Puppies that are disturbed regularly while asleep and are often dragged about tend to grow into neurotic adult dogs. Remember that, above all, your puppy needs rest, regularity, and a whole lot of sleep during the first few weeks.

## Crate

One of the most useful things you can buy for your puppy is a crate which can be used as a room kennel. A (portable) crate is the ideal place for your dog to sleep, because the walls make it feel protected and secure. Good, sturdy crates are not cheap, but if you buy one that allows for growth, you will profit from it for years. You can also use the crate in the car, which is definitely safer than transporting a dog unconfined on the back seat. Another advantage of a crate is that, no matter how far from home you may be, your dog has its familiar sleeping place at hand. However, the most important aspect of a crate is that you can confine your dog for a moment when you have no time to watch it. Mentally healthy dogs do not soil their own sleeping place, nor will your Labrador have the chance to damage your household effects while in the crate. Then you will not have to scold it, and that is good for your mutual relationship. If a crate is introduced in a good, positive manner, i.e. not as a punishment, your dog will gladly seek out its kennel on its own to sleep or rest .

## The first night

A crate is the right place for your puppy to spend the night. Give your pup the chance to relieve itself once more as late as possible at night, and remove the water and food trays. If your puppy was accustomed to relieving itself on newspapers at the breeder's, you

***This brush is a nice toy***

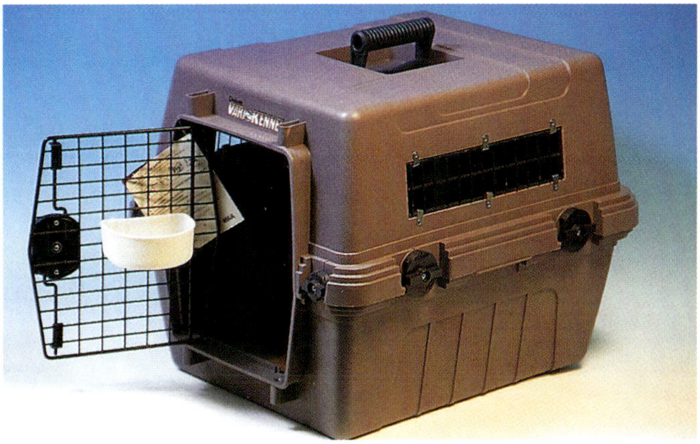

*A crate is a must for successful upbringing and house-training*

can place a newspaper in the corner of the crate. If the crate is not large enough, you can make an enclosure yourself out of spot-welded wire netting. You can then place newspapers outside the crate, inside the netting. Many puppies cry the first and sometimes the second night. They miss their mother and litter mates, and hate being left alone. Since your puppy must learn that it has to be alone every now and then, it is better to ignore this crying and whining completely. If you respond to this "assembly" call, your dog will learn that it does not have to be alone if it makes a lot of noise. In principle, it does not matter whether you console it, yell angrily from your bed, or punish it. It wanted contact, and that is what it got. If you respond, then you increase the chance that your dog will make a racket every time it does not want to be alone, even as an adult. It will not only do so at night, but will also make known its displeasure in the daytime by barking and whining when you have to go out shopping. In order to prevent persistent problems, you must now persevere; once the wrong behavior has been learned, it is very difficult to unlearn. It is helpful to wrap the rag with the scent of the litter around a warm, metal, baby's hot water bottle. The warmth and the surrounding scent of the litter will help your puppy to fall asleep faster.

*Young, yellow Labrador Retriever puppy*

# 6 House-training

## The first steps

Until a puppy is able to eat by itself, the mother dog cleans up the feces and urine of her litter. If the run or kennel where the puppies grow up is large enough, you will seldom find feces in the litter sleeping place. A mentally healthy dog never soils its own sleeping place, since this goes against its natural instinct. It is different when the puppies are kept in too small a space. They are then forced to dirty their nest. If this is not cleaned up quickly enough by the breeder, the pups will get used to a dirty environment. Such puppies are very difficult to house train. In normal cases, however, all puppies are clean by nature. The only thing they have to learn is that your entire house, and that of others, must be considered as a "nest."

Because young puppies cannot completely control their bladders, "accidents" are inevitable up to the age of five to six months.

## The nasal organ

Labradors have an excellent nose and, like all dogs, are creatures of habit. They have an outstanding ability to distinguish the smell of previously made urine puddles or feces, even through the permeating smell of cleaning agents. This also explains why dogs first sniff and turn around before doing their business. Dogs prefer to find the same places for

*Most dogs quickly accept a crate as a safe place to which they can retreat*

*Far right: Labradors have a good nose*

*Young black bitch*

repeat performances. Prevent your dog from developing unclean habits by discouraging it as much as possible from having accidents in the house. If you see your puppy sniffing and turning around, pick it up and put it where it needs to be. Do not call it to go outside, because the urge may become too great on the way out. If you are unable to pay attention for a short time, use the crate, in which your dog will always be clean within its biological possibilities. You can assume in principle that a puppy will have an urge as soon as it wakes up and has eaten. In the beginning, it would definitely not be going too far to allow your puppy to go out at least once an hour. Give it the chance to relieve itself again as late as possible at night, and be there straightaway in the morning to let it out once again. The shorter the night, the greater the chance of success.

## Reward and punishment

Your puppy recognizes its own smells outside, just like in the house. Let it out as much as possible in the same place during the first few weeks. Never forget to reward your pup in a high and friendly voice if it does something outside, repeating this praise on each occasion. If your puppy has an accident in the house, do not make an issue of it. If you punish your Labrador puppy in the act, it will get the idea that you do not want it to relieve itself in your sight. The result is that your puppy will only relieve itself if it is sure that you are not around or are not looking. This makes house-training very difficult, because the pup will certainly do nothing while on the leash, but once home will look for a quiet place behind the sofa. Subsequent punishment is not good. A dog associates both punishment and reward with what it is doing at the moment, and therefore does not understand at all why you are punishing it for what it considers to be no reason. Finally, it is not particularly civilized to "rub its nose" in what it has done. Your puppy understands absolutely none of this. All these forms of punishment cause a sensitive puppy to fear the owner. Even less sensitive dogs can in time develop house-training disorders which are difficult to resolve. You can house-train your dog quickly and without problems without ever having to punish it. It is sufficient to reward it if it does well and to prevent accidents in the house as far as possible.

***Punishment in the act results in "secretly" doing its business***

The sudden occurrence of accidents often has a medical cause, such as diabetes, a kidney disorder, or bladder infection. Always have such a dog examined by a veterinary surgeon.

## Relieving itself on request

Your Labrador Retriever can easily be taught to relieve itself "on request." Excrement on the sidewalk is a source of annoyance for many people, which results in an increasingly severe municipal policy with respect to dogs, of which you and other dog owners are the victims. By teaching your puppy that it may only relieve itself in certain permissible places, you will give non-dog-lovers no more reason to complain. In practice, this means that you will first have to go to a designated dog walking place or dog toilet, so that you can then walk your dog without having to worry that something might still happen.

*You can easily teach your puppy to defecate upon request*

You teach your puppy this request by repeating the word you use for it over and over again when your dog defecates or urinates. It does not matter what word you use, as long as it sounds different from any of the commands. In the first few weeks, you will say that word whenever your puppy relieves itself (outside) on its own initiative; later, you can take it to a dog walking area and say the word as it sniffs about. Never forget to reward your puppy enthusiastically if it actually does something. We know from experience that dogs understand this request within a few months and that it is sufficient to say the word in a place where they are allowed to relieve themselves.

## Emotions

*Three Labrador bitches in different colors*

There are a few situations in which you cannot do anything to your puppy if it releases some urine. With intense emotions, for example when you come home, your puppy can be so happy that it loses control of its bladder. It is senseless to punish your puppy, because it is hardly aware of this and cannot prevent it. Dogs often grow out of this phase.

Another situation is when you are punishing your puppy. If your puppy is strongly affected by your scolding, it will make itself as small as possible and might also release some urine. This is not lack of house-training. Your puppy is using its own language (it has not mastered yours) to try to stop your aggression. It is the most extreme submissive gesture available to a dog.

Submissive urination occurs mainly in puppies that are shy by nature, in combination

with a too dominant owner and/or an inconsistent or too Spartan upbringing.

***Black male***

# 7 ORDER OF RANK AND BODY LANGUAGE

## Pack behavior

Your dog is descended from the wolf and still has many characteristics in common with its ancestor. A strict order of rank applies in a wolf pack, with the "Alpha" (leader of the pack) at the head. The leader of the pack is the most intelligent and often also the strongest wolf which, through his or her strength and correct judgment, increases the pack's chance of survival. The Alpha wolf has many privileges in return for its good services to the pack. It may stand, lie, and walk anywhere; the rest make way promptly. When it growls in order to discipline the pack, this is respected. It may also bite its subordinates, but the other way round is absolutely forbidden. Wolves do well with such leadership.

*A shy puppy*

***Right:* The determination of rank is important if you want to remain the boss in your own house**

For your puppy, the family is the pack and you are the leader of the pack. Just like its forefathers, it feels safe and happy when it experiences consistent leadership with clearly defined limits. A dog that is dominant by nature and receives insuffi-

cient leadership may decide to appoint itself leader of the pack. Your Labrador will then decide, for example, when you may or may not sit on the sofa, when it is time to play, and when and how long you may pet it. It will growl at you or correct you with a bite if you do not obey or if you break the rules. This is very natural behavior for which the dog cannot be blamed; the fault is with the owner, who has not given the dog the leadership it so badly needs. Caring for the coat in such a case is difficult or impossible, because that will put the dog in a subordinate position with respect to the one doing the grooming, i.e. you. Walking on the street is no picnic with a hard pulling dog that decides by itself where to walk and how fast. Off the leash, there is no control whatsoever.

It goes without saying that you must be the one to take on the role of the pack leader and that your dog must always have the lowest rank in the family. There are several rules for this which are fairly easy to apply.

## Rules for determination of rank

The following rules for determination of rank provide clarity, for the puppy as well as the adult dog. If these rules are applied consistently, the dog will understand that it has the lowest rank in your family, so that problems of hierarchy will be prevented in advance.

*Adult yellow male*

*Do not give the dog free access to the entire house*

- This privilege is reserved for the other family members, because they rank higher than the dog. Certain rooms in the house are always taboo.

*Only feed the dog after everyone has eaten*

- Those higher in rank always eat first. You can also feed your dog at other times than your own mealtimes.

*Do not pet or play with the dog if it tries to compel you to do so*

- It commands you to pay attention to it, and therefore gives itself a higher rank: the pack leader decides when playing or petting takes place and for how long.

*Never lie on the floor, but always hold your face higher than the dog's head*

- A higher-ranking dog never takes a lower position than a lower-ranking one; pay attention to this when you sit on the sofa – the dog could soon be "bigger" than its owner.

*Never let your dog "win" at games*

- You do not use its toys, but in outdoor games (retrieving, searching) you use separate toys which you put away after playing. Do not give them to the dog, for then it will have "beaten" you.

*Always walk in front; the dog will follow you*

- Do not allow your dog to determine where you will walk, or be the first out the front door, or the first to enter a room. The leader of the pack always walks in front; the lower-ranked members must follow the leader.

***This gentle facial expression speaks volumes***

## Children and order of rank

Children and Labrador Retrievers are usually an outstanding combination. Nevertheless, things can sometimes go wrong, mainly through an owner's ignorance. To prevent the relationship between your children and the dog from being disturbed, teach your children that they:

- must always call the dog to them and never walk or crawl to it;
- must leave the dog alone when it is eating or sleeping;
- should not give any commands without the supervision of an adult;
- should not lie on the ground, but always hold their face higher than the dog's head;
- should never look the dog directly in its eyes.

If you have very young children, you will not be able to teach them all this at first. In such a situation, see to it that the dog and child are never alone together. Your Labrador is known for its ability to take things in its stride with respect to children, but this does not mean that it can and should tolerate everything. Therefore, supervision is always necessary, for the well-being of the children as well as the dog.

***A submissive dog keeps its tail between its legs and its ears pointed backward***

## "Read" your dog

*A happy, uncomplicated, "average" dog*

In the daily interaction you have with your dog, it is necessary to be able to "read" its behavior: in other words, to understand the meaning of its various actions. For example, it is important for you to know in a certain situation whether your dog is showing dominant or submissive behavior. We shall examine several expressions of dominance and submission, to help you learn to recognize these.

*Body language*

Body language can be observed very well during a meeting, for example with a person or another dog. A dominant attitude of the body is characterized by a tail carried high and pointed ears. The dog stands "high" on its legs and also holds its head high. In order to emphasize its status with respect to another dog, it may lay its head on top of the back, neck, or head of the other dog. In response to this, the other dog will often lick the bottom of the higher-ranked dog's mouth. If your dog licks the bottom of your chin, it is saying: "I am lower in rank, you are the boss." A dog that is uncertain about the situation and considers itself to be of a lower rank will make its body small. It holds its head low, with the ears pointing backward, and also carries its tail low. In meetings with much more dominant dogs or people, or in threatening confrontations, such a dog will keep its tail between its back legs and even roll over on its back and release some urine, the latter being the most extreme form of submission.

*Urination and defecation*

Urine and feces have an important function in mutual social relations between dogs. Other dogs can tell a lot from the scent as well as the place and height where the feces and urine have been deposited-among other things, the social status of the donor. Dominant dogs place their urine scent marks as high as possible: the higher the marker, the more dominant the messenger. The same applies to the feces, which a basically dominant dog will deposit on molehills or other noticeable and higher places. Bitches usually squat to urinate, but very dominant ladies sometimes lift their leg. After a dominant dog has urinated or defecated, it will scratch the ground vigorously. This is also a way to spread scent. Dogs that are by nature more submissive do not spend as much time on their urine and feces. The male lifts his leg hardly at all or only to normal height and often does not scratch the ground afterward.

***The more dominant the dog, the higher it lifts its leg***

*Yes boss, I hear you, but I'm busy at the moment*

# 8 Upbringing

## Socialization

After the imprinting phase, a phase in which puppies make their first acquaintance with the world around them, comes the socialization phase. This phase lasts from the age of about seven weeks until the puppies are twelve to fourteen weeks old. After the imprinting phase, the socialization phase is the most important in a dog's life. As he grows older, your puppy will react calmly to anything it experiences as non-threatening during the socialization phase.

*Eating together makes friends*

**Socialization in practice**

Let your puppy get acquainted in a positive way with as many situations, people, and other animals as possible. Do not place too much emphasis on new situations, but introduce them indirectly as something normal and matter-of-fact. For instance, take your puppy to a shop with automatic sliding doors and ignore it if it hesitates or is frightened; just keep on walking and tug on the leash to encourage your pup to do the same. You can show your puppy that you are self-confident in a variety of situations. Do not react any differently than you would without your dog. Your puppy will then adopt your casu-

*Right: A friendly, open look*

al, self-assured attitude. Think ahead. If you do not have any cats yourself, socialize your pup with a friendly cat. Your dog will live for ten years or more and your life could change quite a lot in that period. A possible new partner could be a cat lover, or perhaps your child will become one. Things such as bridges, elevators, and public transport also belong in this category.

Much socialization will take place unconsciously. If you live in a busy city, your dog will automatically get used to hustle and bustle, car traffic, and other people. You will not have to make any extra effort for that. In such a case, take the puppy to a

rural area, where it can gain impressions of cattle and farm machinery. Whatever happens, make good use of the socialization period, because good socialization can prevent behavioral problems that will be difficult to correct in the future.

> Do not make the mistake of giving your puppy too many impressions at a stretch. This confuses puppies, making them insecure, and can have a negative impact.

**Negative experiences during the socialization phase**

Negative incidents that frighten your puppy during the socialization phase may have a negative effect on its attitude toward similar situations for the rest of its life, although this does not have to be the case. Your puppy sees you as its most important example and your reaction to what happens is decisive for it. If something bad happens, it is very important for you to act in the right way. Also, if your puppy is bitten by another dog or has another traumatic experience, you should react as matter-of-factly as possible. Through this, the event will make less of an impression and will be forgotten more quickly. If, on the other hand, you make an issue of it, for example by panicking,

*Making the acquaintance of such an overconfident young stallion is something you should avoid during the socialization period*

comforting your pup, or picking it up, the incident will remain etched in its memory. So you should never do this, because it will ultimately result in a dog which is full of complexes and difficult to live with. A statement such as: "My dog does not dare go into an elevator, because it got stuck between the doors when it was a puppy" does not hold water. It is not so much the incident itself as the reaction of the owner that largely determines how the dog will react in the future.

*Is your Labrador allowed on the sofa?*

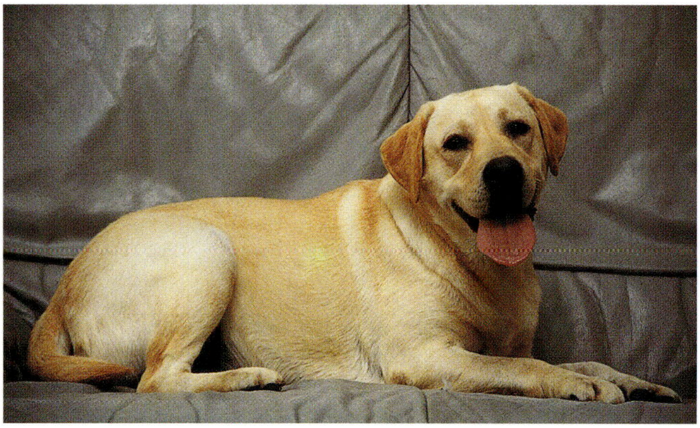

## Consistency

The key to an obedient and happy dog is being consistent with it, not just during its upbringing, but throughout the dog's life. You can do everything "by the book," but this will not do any good if you apply flexible rules. You will have to agree in advance what the dog will and will not be allowed to do. If you decide that the dog is allowed on the sofa, you will also have to accept this when its paws are muddy, and, if it is not allowed on the sofa, do not allow it as an exception if your children pester you to do so. The same holds, for example, for jumping on people. If this does not bother you when you are wearing an old jogging suit, do not forbid it either when you are elegantly dressed and about to go to a reception. Your Labrador will not understand such subtle differences.
Many dogs that are handled inconsistently constantly ignore the commands of their owner. Other, shier dogs will become anxious and insecure. Being consistent is far from easy and will demand much adjustment on your part but also on the part of any other members of your household. Your efforts will, however, be richly rewarded by a happy, obedient dog that knows where your – and therefore its – boundaries lie and will not cross them.

# Clarity in reward and punishment

In order to bring up your dog properly, you must reward it if it does something you would like to be repeated and punish it for undesirable behavior. It is important for the dog to know why it is being rewarded or punished. However easy and simple this may seem, in practice we see that a casual pet and a mumbled "Good dog" are the rule rather than the exception when the dog obeys. Always reward it exuberantly and with enthusiasm. Use a high, cheerful voice and give the dog a sincere hug. You can tell by your dog's reaction if it has really understood the reward. Its whole body and face should radiate happiness. The same applies to punishment. If you always say "phooey," and do nothing else, your puppy will learn that you just say something frequently and will not pay much attention to it. In order to ensure that your dog experiences the punishment as such, you should use the lowest possible voice and say convincingly and angrily: "Bad dog!" or, "No!" Most puppies will understand this very well. You might sometimes have to back up your words in order to convince a less sensitive dog that you mean business. You could then, for example, throw an object at the dog or give it a good tug on the leash.

*Glowing with pride: The reward has been clearly understood*

**Good timing**

In addition to knowing that it is being rewarded or punished, it is just as important for your dog to know why this is happening. Therefore, you should neither reward your dog before it has properly obeyed a command, nor delay the reward afterward.

Imagine this situation: you give your puppy a command and see that it is about to obey it. Do not reward it yet, but immediately after it has obeyed the command. Good timing is also important for punishment. Your dog always associates punishment and reward with what it is doing at that moment in time. If your dog has made a mess while you were away and you punish it when you come home, perhaps hours later, it will not understand this at all. The shredded newspapers, the puddle on your carpet, or the chewed-up cloth have been long forgotten. According to the dog, the situation is as follows: you come

home, it runs happily to greet you, and you then punish it. The connection made by the puppy is: When my owner comes home, I get punished. It remembers that and, the next time you come home, will take on a fearful, dejected attitude in advance. Such an attitude is too often considered as "acting guilty," which definitely is not the case.
If you have a puppy that often breaks things while you are away, use the crate. By not giving your dog the chance to do anything wrong, it will have always been "good" when you come home and that is beneficial for the mutual relationship.

## Choke chains and hunting ropes

There are several types of choke chain, with very thin or large links, and there are choke collars of nylon, leather, and cotton. The last-mentioned is often used for hunting dogs such as the Labrador Retriever, and they are called "hunting ropes" (see photo, p. 63 top).

***When you punish your dog, it must know why this is happening***

The purpose of such a choke chain is to enable you to mimic a "correction bite" by tugging on the leash. A correction bite is a bite given by a higher-ranking wolf or dog to a lower-ranking member of the pack if it does not obey or does something the higher-ranking member disapproves of. If you correct it in the right way, your dog will know exactly what you mean and will act accordingly. This is on condition that the chain or rope is placed properly around the neck. The end of the chain (to which the clasp is fastened) should be at the top of the neck. When you do this, the chain will open if it is not being pulled. In addition to verbal punishment in a low, angry voice, correction by a properly measured pull on the choke chain is the right way to correct your half or fully

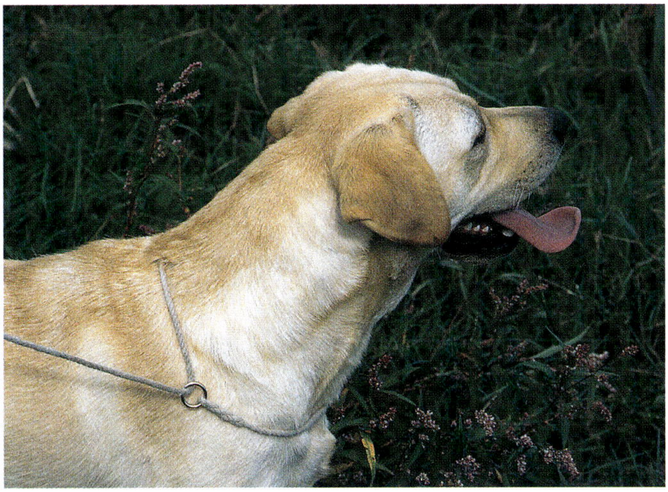

*A hunting rope, just like a choke chain, is an ideal way to imitate a correction bite*

grown dog. Other forms of correction, such as shaking the skin of the neck, hitting with a newspaper, and suchlike, should never be used. The only thing you will achieve by this is to make your dog afraid of you, because it does not understand such punishments.

*Choke chain*

# 9 Basic training

## Getting accustomed to a collar and leash

Before you can begin to teach commands or walk down the street, your puppy will have to get accustomed to a collar and learn to walk on a leash. Buy a well-fitting, soft, but sturdy collar. A puppy can worm his way out of a collar that is too big or

*Most Labradors learn quickly to walk on a leash*

too loose, and this could lead to dangerous situations on the street. If you put the collar on just before you feed your puppy or before you go with him into the garden, your pup will pay less attention to it and get used to it sooner. Once your puppy has become accustomed to the collar, you can attach a leash to it. First, let your puppy walk around by himself with the leash, thus becoming used to its weight. Later, you can hold the leash and exercise gentle pressure to encourage your puppy to walk with you. Do not pull the leash and do not drag your pup behind you, but entice him to come along with an inviting voice, possibly supported by treats.

## Tips for a successful upbringing

*Right: "Stay" in a ditch; the epitome of obedience*

**Be consistent**

Consistency should be practiced at all times, including during training. Do not go back on a command given ear-

lier and do not be satisfied with a half-obeyed command. Close off a session with a well-followed command.

**You release the command, not your puppy**
If you tell your pup to sit and he blithely gets up and walks away after a few seconds, he has then lifted your command on his own. Your puppy should not be allowed to do this; you lift the command yourself by saying "at ease" or "all right" in good time.

**Do not be too demanding**
Your Labrador puppy is playful and easily distracted. Sitting or lying in place without moving for five minutes cannot yet be demanded of him. Release the command after a few seconds and expand it gradually. Then he will not be tempted to be disobedient.

**Keep your puppy motivated**
A puppy that enjoys being trained will learn faster and more permanently. Therefore, do not train for too long a time at once; five to ten minutes a day is long enough to start with. Alternate the commands with play and never forget to reward your dog enthusiastically if he does something well. Nothing motivates a puppy better than an owner who is obviously satisfied with him.

*"Were you talking to me?"*

- **Be clear**
  Express your commands clearly and say his name first, so that your puppy knows you are talking to him.

- **Choose the right moment**
  Do not train if your puppy has just eaten, has a full bladder, or is sleepy. Only give a command when his attention is focused on you. If he is distracted, you know in advance that he will hardly be aware of your command. Training should therefore be done in a quiet place, where there is as little distraction as possible.

- **Avoid unnecessary repetition**
  A puppy that hears the following when he has to sit: "Max sit, sit down Max, no, sit, I mean it, sit Max, sit," will learn that he can ignore numerous commands. Unfortunately, commands such as "here" are given too often in this way. A command repeated several times in a short period of time loses its force. Attract your puppy's attention by first saying his name and give the command once only, loud and clear, when you know for sure that you have his undivided attention.

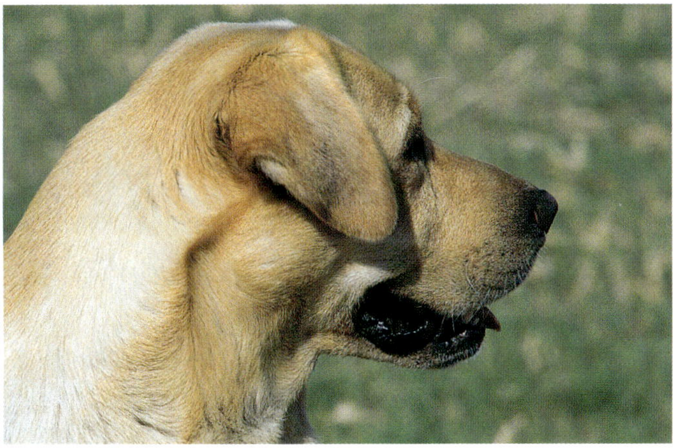

***Is it focusing on something else? First, draw its attention***

## Come here on command

The first command you can teach your puppy is to come to his owner on command. When you say in a cheerful and loud voice: "Max, here!," your puppy must come to you forthwith in a straight line. To practice this, you can put a long leash on your pup. Let your puppy sniff about and play, and see to it that he does not expressly notice that you are holding the end of the leash. Call his name, followed by the

*If your puppy comes to you, it is always a good dog*

command "Here!" Back up your command by squatting and hitting the ground invitingly with your hands. If your puppy responds by coming to you, give him a hug and a treat. If he does not respond and you know he heard you, repeat the command and give the leash a short tug to back this up. If you have good contact with your puppy and make it as interesting as possible to come to you and stay (with friendly words, a hug, and a treat), he will learn this command very quickly. If he has obeyed the command well, play with him before putting on the leash. If you do not do this, the puppy will learn that "Here!" means "the fun is over," while being with the owner should make him feel good. If your puppy knows this command well, you can practice it further in a safe and fenced-in place without having to put him on the leash.

**The self-willed adolescent**

About the time your Labrador has reached puberty, this command can give rise to problems. Your dog can make a game of it and run increasingly further away as a challenge to you to follow him. Do not do this. If your dog does not respond to your command, squat, walk in the opposite direction, hide, or throw something at him to frighten him. Most dogs react to this by quickly finding their owner. When your dog finally comes to you after a long period of urging, reward him with as much enthusiasm as otherwise and give him a treat. Punishment is associated with precisely what the dog is doing at that moment; in this case, he is obeying your command.

## Sitting on command

It is easy to teach a Labrador Retriever puppy to sit on command. By holding a treat right above his nose and giving the command "Sit, he will often sit by himself. If he does not yet understand completely what you mean, encourage him to take the proper position by pressing his hindquarters lightly with your free hand. Give him the treat as soon as he sits and

*"Sit" with the aid of a treat*

*Sitting at the curb*

do not forget to praise him verbally.
It is advisable to teach your puppy to sit at each curb during a walk, even if no cars are coming. Once a puppy has been taught to do this consistently, he will know that a curb is a boundary which he simply cannot cross without your command "Come on!"

## Lying down on command

The command "Down" can be taught very well with a treat. Teach your dog this command from a sitting position. If your puppy is sitting, hold a treat in front of his nose in your clenched fist and move your fist downward, while giving the command "Down." Your pup will follow the delicious smell automatically with his nose and, if you then exercise light pressure on his back with your free hand, he will understand

roughly what you expect of him. The lower your dog goes, the more you open your hand. If the puppy lies down, you open your hand completely and give the treat. You can encourage your pup during the exercise, but he is only a "Good dog" when it actually lies down.

## Staying on command

The command "Stay" means that your dog remains lying, sitting, or standing in the same place he was when the command was given. The most practical way to teach your dog at first is to have him do this from a sitting position. You can extend this command later. Put your dog on the leash and let him sit to your left. Give the command "Stay." Then take a step forward or to the side, and make sure the leash is hanging loosely. If your pup continues to sit, reward him immediately. If he stands up straightaway, or crawls in your direction, say "No!," and have your pup sit again in the same place. Then give the command and step away again.

*"Sit" and "Stay"*

*A puppy should also be able to have fun*

*This puppy has mastered the command "stay"*

*Teach your Labrador as quickly as possible not to pull on the leash*

It is important precisely for this command to release your puppy promptly by saying "At ease" or "OK." "Staying" is no simple task for a young pup. If you release the command promptly, your puppy will not have to be disobedient.
You can build up this exercise by stepping increasingly further away from your pup; ultimately, you will be able to practice this for a longer time and without the leash.

## "Place"

One command that you can teach very early is "Place." The purpose of this command is to have the dog go immediately to his basket or crate. It is best to practice this when your puppy is a bit tired. If he has just woken up or is busily playing, he will definitely be less motivated. Put him in his place while giving the command "Place." If your puppy remains in his basket or crate, regardless of whether he is standing, sitting, or lying, he is a "Good dog" and you may certainly let him know that. If he immediately starts to walk away, say "No!," repeat the command, and put him back in his place. If your puppy understands what you expect from him, it will subsequently suffice to say "Max, place" and point to his basket or kennel. Later on, you can also teach your puppy to go to his place when you are somewhere else. Always take along the same blanket when you go visiting. You can lay the blanket there and send your dog to his temporary place.

## Enjoying a walk together

Labrador Retrievers love to take walks. They set the pace and sometimes drag their owner behind them. As you know, it is not a good sign when your dog decides where to walk together and how fast. Such decisions are taken by the pack leader: thus, by you. From the beginning, you must correct tugging at the leash in a clearly defined manner. You do this by giving the choke chain or hunting rope a quick, but strong pull each time your puppy does this. Do not reward him for not pulling. Not pulling on the leash is no special achievement by your dog. Clearly correcting your dog when he pulls will teach him that he has nothing to gain by pulling, except an unpleasant feeling. It is very important here to keep a close eye on your puppy from a very young age. An adult dog that has not been properly, or perhaps never, corrected is so accustomed to pulling on the leash that he does not know any better, and by this time will have also become very strong.

## Training devices

Some Labrador Retrievers have what are called "insensitive necks." The have a well-muscled neck, pull the owner down the street, and hardly react to correction with a choke chain. A so-called "halti," or "gentle leader," is a solution that enables such Labradors to take relaxed walks with you. These devices look like a horse's muzzle and are not put around the neck but around the head. They both work according to the same principle.

If your dog pulls the leash, the halti will immediately put an unpleasant pressure on the bridge of his nose and will also pull his head downward to one side. You play a minimal part in this; these devices have a self-correcting effect. If your dog does not pull, he does not feel any discomfort at all and will teach himself not to pull. A wide range of both devices are available at pet shops.

***A halti, or gentle leader, as worn by this young male, is a solution for dogs with insensitive necks.***

# 10 Care

## Basket or crate

The best thing you can buy for your new housemate is a spacious crate. If you buy a kennel that allows for growth, you and your Labrador will enjoy it for years. If you would rather have a basket, your first choice should be a dog stretcher or a sturdy plastic basket. The disadvantage of cushions, soft materials, or plush baskets is that many puppies try out their teeth on them. Once your puppy has discovered how much fun it is to chew such a basket to pieces, this could become an annoying habit that persists even when the dog is older. As a fully-grown dog, however, your Labrador will benefit from a soft place to lie, because it can get ugly calluses on its elbows from a hard surface. While your dog is still young, not giving it the opportuni-

*A suitable basket is always somewhat removed from the floor*

*A dog cushion is ideal for older animals*

*Far right: Yellow male*

ty to get into the bad habit of destroying a basket will benefit you for years to come.
You can lay a blanket in the kennel or basket, which you wash regularly and shake out every day.

## Collars and leashes

In order to walk your dog, you need a well-fitting leather or nylon dog collar, a long leash, and possibly a retractable leash. You would do better to buy a collar that fits well at present, rather than one that is too big with room for growth. Your Labrador can easily worm its way out of a collar that is too

*Nylon collars are soft, but exceedingly strong*

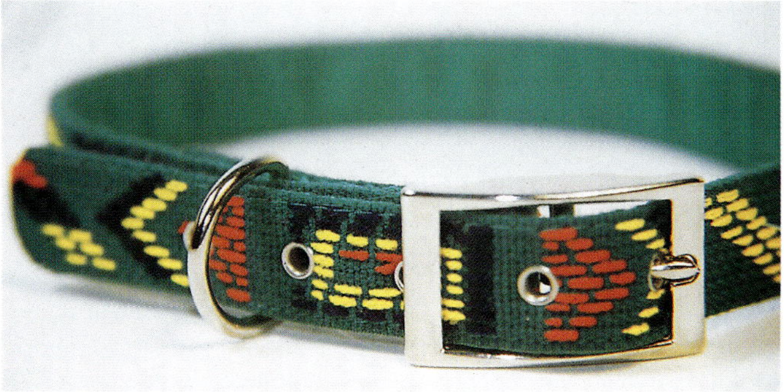

loose. An ordinary leather or a thicker nylon leash is quite sufficient. The advantage of a nylon leash over an average quality leather one is that it is stronger, lasts longer, and is easier to clean when necessary. A leash of about five feet (one and a half meters) long is sufficient, but if you want to give your dog more freedom of movement, the various retractable leashes which you can find at any pet shop are ideal.
Ordinary collars are not as suitable for training and upbringing. You would do better to buy a separate hunting rope or a thin choke chain. Because the hairs on your Labrador's neck can be damaged if a choke chain is worn too often, you should use it only for training.

## Food and drink bowls

Many different kinds of food and drink bowls can be bought, in all sizes, shapes, and prices. If you want the bowls to last for a long time, choose stainless steel versions. These are practically indestructible, very easy to clean, and, if necessary, can be boiled. Special stands are available to prevent these bowls from sliding. Adjustable height stands are very handy in practice, because they can be adjusted to a comfortable eating height as your dog grows.

## Grooming the coat

To groom your Labrador's coat, you need a rubber massage brush or glove, and a brush with metal pins. Plastic-covered pins are preferable because they spare the skin. You can brush your dog's coat about once a week with the metal brush to remove loose hairs and flakes. During the shedding period, it is better to use the rubber brush or glove, because the rough surface of the rubber removes the dead hairs faster and more effectively from the coat.
A weekly brushing is not just necessary to groom the coat. You massage the skin at the same time, which improves circulation. Brushing also strengthens the mutual bond and any parasites, wounds, or other disorders are discovered more quickly. The breed standard prescribes a so-called "otter's tail" with a rounded tip. If your Labrador has longer hairs at

***Accustom your dog to grooming at an early age***

the tip of its tail or even a tassel, round it off neatly with sharp scissors.

**Bathing**

Labrador Retrievers have a water-resistant coat. A thin layer of oil on the hairs keeps the skin as dry as possible, even

*This Labrador will soon need a bath*

during swimming. Although your Labrador will get itself really dirty every now and then, as a general rule you will not have to bathe it often. Mud becomes sand when it dries, which can easily be brushed out of the coat. If the dog has to be bathed once in a while, always use a special dog shampoo. Shampoo for people removes the oil layer from the coat and skin.

## Care of the nails

Long nails are not only ugly, they can be very troublesome to a dog. Nails that are too long break more easily and, furthermore, your dog will develop a different (incorrect) gait, because its long nails make it impossible to walk normally.

By regularly clipping the points of your dog's nails, and continuing to do so if necessary, you will prevent your Labrador's nails from becoming (too) long. If the nails are never clipped, the "quick" grows along with them. The ultimate result of this is that the nails can never again be clipped to the proper length without hurting your dog. Do not use scissors, but always use good quality nail clippers especially for dogs. Do

*Clipping the nails*

not forget the thumbnails. These are on the inside of the legs, just above the paws.

**Winter nose**

Black and yellow Labradors have a black nose, and that of chocolate dogs is liver-colored. If you have a yellow Labrador that normally has a black nose, you will notice that the black color every now and then becomes somewhat pinkish. This happens mainly during cold seasons and sometimes also in the heat period. This phenomenon is called "winter nose" or "snow nose." A winter nose is a completely normal pheno-

*The noses of yellow Labradors can change color*

menon in the yellow colors. Sooner or later, all yellow Labradors develop a permanently lighter-colored nose, although one dog might develop this somewhat earlier than another. Yellow dogs born with little pigment, the so-called "yellow-livers," always have a light-colored nose.

## Care of the teeth

Your puppy's milk teeth will be replaced by permanent, adult teeth from the age of four months. This period of change lasts about two months. Because some dogs are really bothered by the process, they sometimes eat less than usual. During this period, many puppies have an increased need to chew, and you can meet your dog's need by giving it various articles designed for this purpose.

It sometimes happens that a milk tooth will not want to loosen, while the permanent tooth is coming through. This can cause the permanent teeth to grow crooked. Keep a close eye on this process. Make it a habit in any case to inspect your dog's teeth once a month. Tartar and plaque can form, especially on the back molars, which if neglected could result in tooth decay and loss of the teeth. You can brush away light plaque yourself with a toothbrush and children's toothpaste. Real tartar is better removed by the veterinarian, but it does not have to come to this. Dogs that can use their teeth regularly on dog biscuits and hard, tough chewing bones keep their teeth healthy and strong for a longer time.

*Milk teeth*

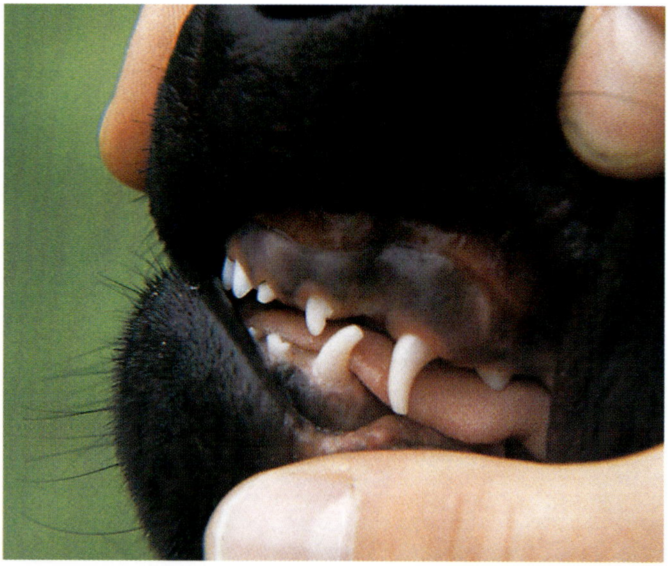

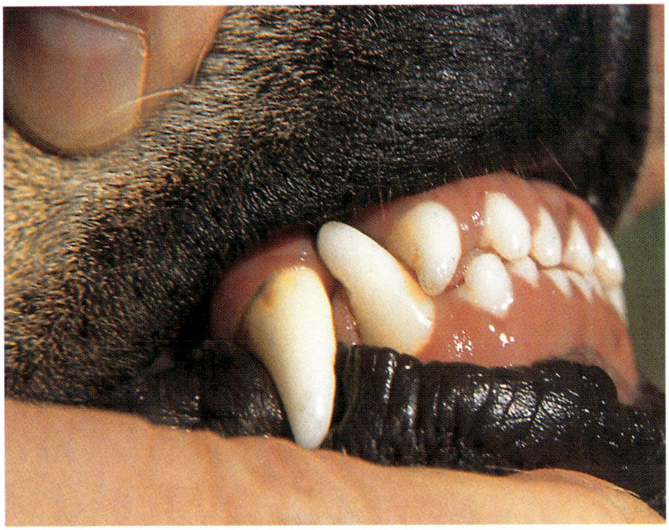

*Adult teeth*

## Care of the ears

The auditory canal of your Labrador Retriever does not have to be cleaned often. If you notice too much ear wax and sand in the ear, remove this with a canine ear cleaner and use a tissue to remove the loose dirt. Because the auditory canal of dogs is not straight but curved, you would do better not to use cotton swabs. They can push the dirt further into the auditory canal, which could cause an inner ear infection.
A dark, stinking, and grainy discharge in the ear is a sign of an ear mite infection. Your veterinarian can give you an effective remedy for this.

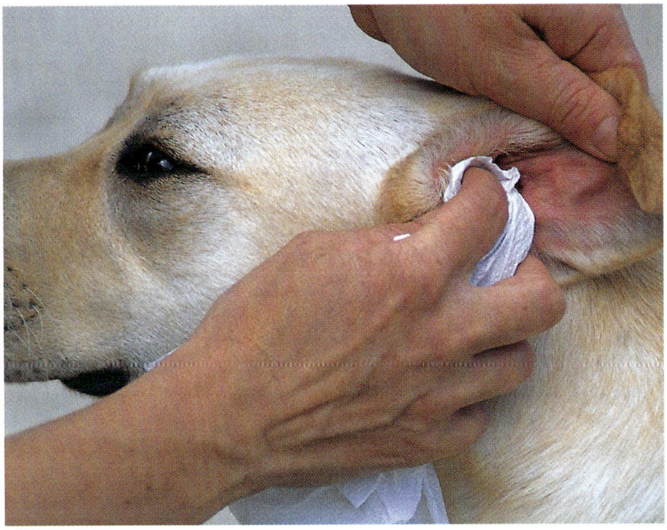

*Cleaning the ears*

## Eye care

Most Labradors do not have problems with dirty eyes, but some dogs suffer from them frequently. This may be due to a (slight) defect in the connection of the eyelids. The somewhat hanging eyelids (ectropion) make them sensitive to dust particles and dirt, through which the eye membrane easily becomes irritated. You can prevent the resulting dark tear marks with a special eye lotion. If your dog has a serious problem with discharge, its eyelids hang loosely, or they are pulled inwards, always contact your veterinarian.

## Vermin

### Combating fleas

Fleas are a nuisance for people and animals. Some Labradors hardly have a problem with them, while others develop an allergy to flea saliva and literally scratch and tear themselves bald after one single flea bite. In order to combat fleas effectively, you must not only treat the dog itself, but also other animals and certainly the surroundings of your dog and places where it often lies. Research has shown that, if the dog has only one flea, ninety-nine others in the egg, larva, or pupa stage are in the immediate vicinity.

Many different anti-flea remedies are available on the market, and some work better than others. Experience will teach which anti-flea remedy is the handiest for you to use and the most effective. Because puppies are very sensitive to aggressive anti-flea remedies, you can better obtain an adjusted remedy from the vet.

### Removing ticks

If you often walk your dog in a natural environment or in the vicinity of bushes and tall grass, there is a chance that your dog could get a tick. Ticks are very small parasites that clamp their mouths to the skin of their host and suck themselves full of blood. Only when they have sucked themselves full are they visible, as big, grey bumps on your dog's skin. Be as careful as possible when removing ticks. If a tick is pulled out of the skin, the jaws remain behind in the skin and can cause infections. Therefore, it is better to remove a tick with special tick tongs, using a twisting motion.

Tick bites can be dangerous; they can transmit the dreaded Lyme's disease. Any means of preventing a tick bite (such as an anti-tick collar) is not an unnecessary luxury.

### Combating worms

There are different types of worms, but roundworms and tape-

worms are the most common in dogs. Almost all puppies are already infected with roundworms at birth. Whether or not the bitch was wormed in time has no effect on the infection of the pups. The breeder should therefore worm a litter several times before the puppies go to their new homes. An intensive worm infection can be dangerous, since large numbers of worms can damage your puppy's organs. If such an extreme worm infection is present, that puppy will clearly be in pain, become thinner, and its stomach will feel hard. A tapeworm infection can be recognized mainly by the segments resembling grains of rice that you find in the excrement. Fleas function as temporary hosts for tapeworms. If your dog has fleas, it could also be infected with a tapeworm. Therefore, always keep to the worming schedule provided by the breeder or the veterinarian. If your dog is fully grown, a wormer every six months is usually sufficient.

***Fleas are a nuisance***

## Vaccinations

There are a number of life-threatening diseases against which you can protect your dog by having it vaccinated. The most well known of these diseases are canine parvovirus, canine distemper, Weil's disease, hepatitis, and leptospirosis. The vaccinations cannot all be given at once to the puppy, but are spread over one to one and a half months. The final puppy vaccination is given at the age of about twelve weeks; before then, your pup will not be fully protected against these diseases.

To prevent the risk of infection, you should avoid walking your dog in places frequented by lots of other dogs until your vet has given the green light. If you regularly take your dog to shows or a dog kennels, a vaccination or nose drops against kennel cough is a good precaution. Kennel cough is very contagious, being transmitted in places where large groups of dogs are housed and bark a lot. Many kennels make this vaccination mandatory in addition to the usual vaccinations.

A vaccination against rabies is mandatory in some areas and generally a legal requirement of taking your dog abroad. It must be administered at least a month in advance and may not be older than a year; some vaccinations may not be older than six months. Upon vaccination, your vet will give you an official form that serves as proof of vaccination and can be shown on official request.

*Periodic vaccinations are necessary to protect your Labrador against fatal diseases*

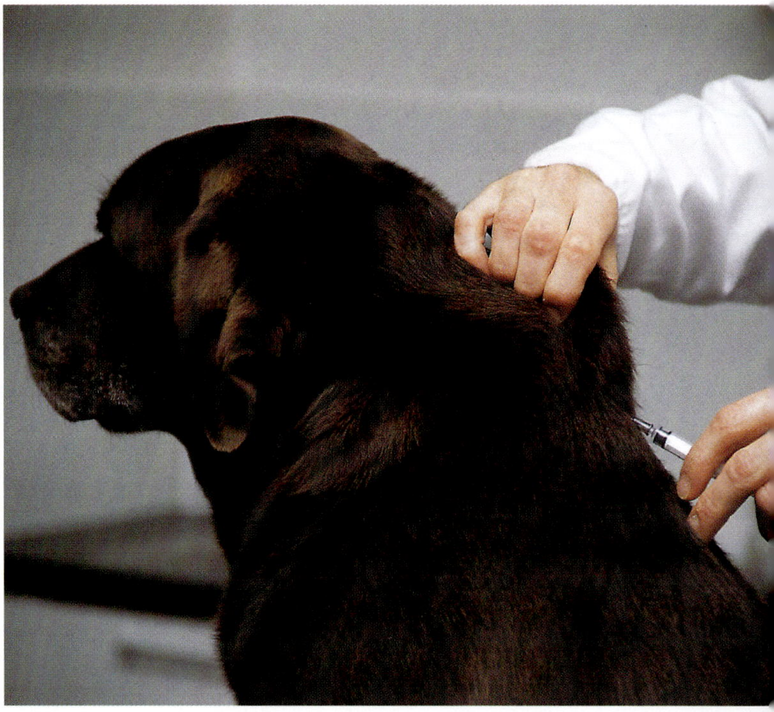

# 11 Feeding

## A dog does not live only on meat

*Right: Chewing on a bone is good for the teeth*

Many people think that a dog is an absolute carnivore, but, just like the wolf, a dog cannot live on a diet of animal protein alone. Scientists who have studied the behavior of wolves have established that they usually eat the entrails of their prey first. Dogs and other predators cannot digest fresh vegetable foods, for which a specially adapted digestive system is necessary, that herbivores do possess. Predators then make use of the adaptations of their prey; the vegetable food present in their entrails is largely "pre-digested," and is therefore easier for the predator to metabolize. Wolves do not only eat the entrails and muscle meat of their prey, but also chew on the bones, which provide their calcium requirement. Therefore, dog food manufacturers not only process meat into their products, but also calcium and (artificially) "pre-digested" vegetable nutrients.

*Expanded dry puppy food*

## Complete foods

There are different types of complete foods, such as dry puppy food, dinners, some canned foods, and complete freezer meals. If it is stated on the packaging that the food is complete, then the manufacturer warrants that the food contains all the vitamins and nutrients that your dog needs. You should not add anything to complete meals, because you will disturb the balance between the nutrients. This applies in particular to calcium. Never add this to a complete food, because too much calcium cannot be excreted. It settles on bones and joints and causes much suffering.
Each complete food has advantages and disadvantages. It is of course fine when your dog likes the food you have chosen, but do not let this influence you too much. If the choice is left to the dog, it would prefer to eat

*Complete dinner with rice*

food rich in fat and salt, and everyone knows that too much of these can never be healthy.

## Incomplete foods

In addition to the complete foods, there are also incomplete foods and simple meat meals available. Incomplete foods are, for example, meatless dinners. You have to add the meat. There are also incomplete canned foods that you must mix with the dinner. Simple meat meals are, for instance, pure chicken and tripe. All these incomplete foods are meant to be mixed. They are neither suitable as, nor intended to be, the only food for a dog. Therefore, take a good look at the packaging to see whether the food is complete or meant to be mixed with other types of food.

## Self-prepared food

Preparing your own dog food is not a simple task. Not only is it important to give your dog sufficient nutrients, but the proportion of vitamins to minerals must also be correct. Too much of a certain nutrient can be harmful and, in the wrong proportions, some ingredients are known to destroy the effect of others. If you would still like to prepare your dog's food yourself, you need to master this complicated matter. Several good books are available on the subject that can help you on your way.

## Diseases and disorders

**Aujeszki**

There is a disease that dogs can contract if they come into

contact with pork. This disease is known as Aujeszki's disease and is fatal for your dog. Therefore, never give your dog fresh pork products. Vaccinations against this disease are available for dogs that regularly come into contact with pigs. These vaccinations, however, do not provide one hundred percent protection for your dog.

### Too fat or too thin

A Labrador Retriever is a broadly-built dog and at first sight always looks somewhat fatter and fuller than other dogs. You must prevent your dog from becoming too fat. Fat dogs do not

***Labradors tend to get fat***

live as long and are more susceptible to heart disease and other disorders than their slimmer congeners. You can easily tell by feeling your dog's ribs whether or not it is too fat or just the right weight. Press the sides of your dog with your fingers. If you can feel your dog's ribs, even if they are not visible, the dog is not too fat. However, if you must press further in order to feel the ribs, you should reduce its food. Labradors that are too fat can often be recognized by the thick fold of skin at the root of the tail.

It is not easy to put your Labrador Retriever on a diet. Labradors love good food, and seldom leave any over. If you find it difficult to give your Labrador less to eat, it can benefit from diet food for dogs that are overweight.

Hardly any Labradors are too thin. Should your dog go through a difficult period, or not want to eat at all, this can have various causes. It could be that your dog has learned that, when it refuses to eat its dry puppy food, you give it something better tasting instead. In such a case, it can do no harm to let your dog fast for a day. It is a different matter when your dog also rejects this food. The cause could be an underlying disease, a painful tooth, or a foreign object in its stomach. In such a case, always have your dog examined by the veterinarian.

Between four and six months, your Labrador exchanges its milk teeth for permanent teeth. In this period, the dog may have less of an appetite, without this doing any harm.

## Puppy food

You have received a list from the breeder stating how much, at what times, and what kind of food you can best give your pup. Because puppies still have such a small stomach, they

> Adult Labrador bitches weigh between 55 and 65 pounds (25 and 30 kilos), males between 65 and 75 pounds (30 and 35 kilos).

*Puppies need several portions of food a day*

cannot eat large quantities of food all at once. The feeding can best be spread throughout the day in small portions. These four or five meals a day can gradually be reduced to two meals for an adult dog.
It is always better to feed your dog twice a day. Smaller portions can be utilized better by the body and are less taxing on the digestive system. In the beginning, you can give your puppy special puppy food, but, when your pup is about four or five months old, you should switch to food for adult dogs. This is certainly true when you give food with a high protein content, which could lead to a disproportionately fast growth. This can cause musculoskeletal disorders and, by growing too fast, your dog may suffer from growing pains. In addition to complete puppy food, you can treat your puppy once a week to a portion of cooked meat, such as beef heart or headcheese. This has a positive effect on the intestinal flora. Instead of cooked meat, you can also give your adult dog fresh tripe.

## Inappropriate food

Not all foods are appropriate for all dogs. One dog will live a long, healthy life on brand X, while another will have too thin bowel movements and become sickly from the same brand. In the first instance, you should keep to the feeding advice obtained from your breeder, who has usually had many years of experience with Labrador Retrievers and has apparently had the best results with the brand or type of food recommended to you. Nevertheless, if you have an idea that this food is not suitable for your dog, for example because of a deviation in color or texture of the feces, unusual shedding or flaking of the skin, or the dog is otherwise out of condition, have your dog examined first by the veterinarian. If the vet cannot find any physical cause, the lack of condition could be an indication that the type or brand of food you give is not (any longer) appropriate for your dog. If you switch to another type of food, accustom your dog gradually to this change by replacing a little more of the old food with the new food each day. A sudden switch could cause diarrhea. You will not notice a rapid change in condition, but after a month or two you should be able to see a difference.

## Chewing articles

To keep your dog's teeth healthy and free of plaque, you must regularly give it something to chew on. This also prevents boredom, which can cause some dogs to chew up things in the house. A tough buffalo hide bone or cooked beef bone of considerable size is very suitable for this. It is better not to give

*Various chewing articles*

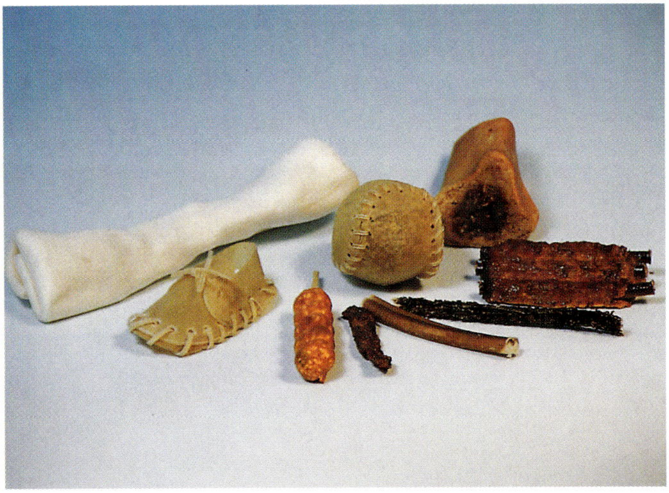

your dog the bones of any fowl, pig, or game. These splinter rather quickly and can injure the digestive system. Marrow bones are also a risk. It sometimes happens that a marrow bone gets stuck fast around the lower jaw.

For a number of years, there have been plastic alternatives to animal chewing bones on the market, that have the same effect as traditional bones but are safer, more hygienic, and last much longer.

*Plastic chewing bone*

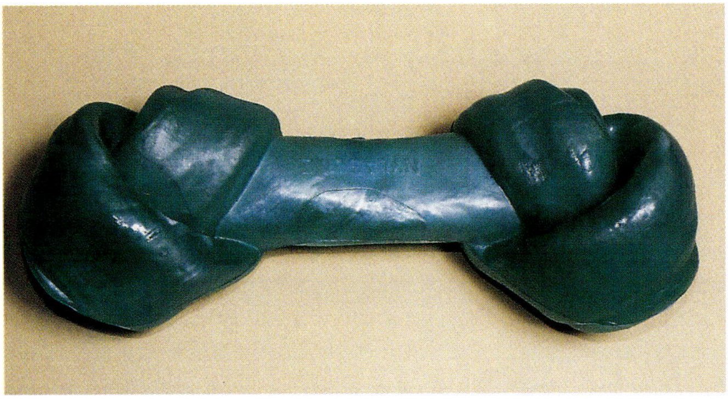

*Fresh drinking water must always be available*

*Older dogs need an adjusted, less protein-rich diet*

# 12 Exercise and Activity

## Measured exercise during the growth phase

A Labrador puppy weighs between 10 and 18 ounces (three hundred and five hundred grams) at birth, but within a year grows into a dog of fifty-five to sixty-five pounds (twenty-five to thirty kilos). This rapid growth is a heavy burden on the musculoskeletal system. A too heavy or incorrect burden

*It is better to let your dog romp about when it is fully grown*

on the ligaments during this growth phase can cause disorders such as hip and elbow dysplasia, which your dog will suffer from for the rest of its life. In order to tax the joints as little as possible, it is important to ensure that your dog does not get too fat.

You should also keep an eye on your growing dog's activities. Young Labrador Retrievers are energetic and rumunctious dogs, that never know when to stop. Prevent your dog from getting tired by not playing with it for too long a time at once and not taking it for long walks. Climbing stairs, jumping, playing with dogs that are bigger and stronger, and slipping on a smooth floor can also damage its body. Protect your puppy, but do not be too careful. Its muscles must be given the chance to develop properly, and will not do so if you wrap your pup in cotton wool. Above all, let it walk straight and take it out several times a day for short distances. You do not have to keep it from frolicking and jumping every now and again, but do not let your puppy overdo things. There will be time enough to walk through the woods and meadows for hours on end later, if your careful nurturing enables your dog to develop a strong body in its first year of life.

*Right: What's there?*

## Scents during the walk

During your daily walks you will notice that your Labrador Retriever stops here and there to sniff some interesting smells. From these scents, including those of the urine and feces of other dogs, your dog gathers information on the situation of the messengers. Your dog will in turn sprinkle some urine or scratch the ground to leave information about itself for other dogs. Scents form a very important part of the communication process between dogs and the daily "walk around the block" is as important to your dog as the news on television is to us. It is therefore unkind to forbid your dog completely to sniff or to spread some information itself, but on the other hand it is not possible to give the dog absolute freedom to do so. Few people appreciate the neighborhood dogs using their garden gate as a communication center, and that is only logical. Also, when training your dog, you should not allow it to be distracted by anything else, including the scents of other dogs. Your pup's undivided attention must be focused on you.

## Safety in the car

If you have a car, your dog will be transported regularly on four wheels. It is better not to transport the dog loosely in the back seat of the car or the passenger's seat. You could then be hindered and, in the event of a collision, your dog would have no protection. You would do better to use a crate or bench for transport by car. If you have an estate car, you can fit a metal

***Two different methods of transporting your dog safely by car***

dog rack between the passenger space and the cargo space. Special seat belts are also sold for dogs.

## Swimming

For years, Labrador Retrievers have been selected for fetching shot game out of the water and bringing it to the hunter. Most Labradors really enjoy retrieving objects from water.

There are very few that do not like to swim. Special "dummies" can be bought that remain afloat on water and are a safe alternative to branches and sticks. (Tennis) balls also float and are an attractive target for your Labrador. Many owners only let their dog swim during the warm seasons, but, with its water-resistant coat and love of anything that is wet, your Labrador should enjoy going into the water during cold and rainy seasons just as much. There is nothing wrong with this, as long as you dry your dog thoroughly when you come home and do not leave it outside or in a drafty place. That would make even a Labrador sick. Be careful where you allow your dog to swim. Waters that are unsafe for people, for example because of treacherous

currents or the presence of disease bacteria, are unsafe for dogs as well. Also pay attention to the area surrounding the swimming water; your dog could get caught in fish nets and also in long, stringy water plants. The shore must slope into the water. A high drop-off forms a difficult or insurmountable obstacle for many dogs. They jump happily into the water, but cannot come back out.

*This Labrador is retrieving a dummy*

## Retrieving

Almost all Labradors have retrieving in their blood. All puppies like to walk about with objects in their mouth, and it is not difficult to teach them to bring these objects to you. If your puppy has something in its mouth, call its name and say very cheerfully "Retrieve!" Because you make inviting gestures, squat down, and encourage it with your voice, your puppy will quickly understand your intention. Reward it enthusiastically when it brings you the object, and give it a treat in return or throw the object so it can retrieve it again. If your dog has something in its mouth that it should not touch, do not be angry with it, but allow it to retrieve it. Then throw an object that it is allowed to have. In the beginning, it is fine whenever your dog brings you something. Later you can expect it to sit properly in front of you and let go of the toy at your command. You can also teach your Labrador to heel and wait until the object has landed and you have given it the command "Retrieve."
For retrieval, you should use a safe toy rather than a branch or stick. Splinters from branches can damage your dog's mouth and digestive tract.

## Searching games

Your Labrador has an excellent nose. There are various games (but also serious activities) for which your Labrador can and must use its nose. For instance, you could hide its favorite toy under a pail and let the dog find it. You should not make this too difficult in the beginning, for your dog needs to understand what the intention is. You can expand on this later, for example by turning more pails upside down so that your dog must find the pail under which you have hidden its ball or toy. You can also fix a wash line at your Labrador's eye level and hang several rags on it. You have kept two rags in your pocket for a while, so that they have picked up a specific scent that your dog recognizes. One of the rags is then hung between the "odorless" rags on the wash line. Let your dog sniff the other rag and then point to the wash line to encourage it to find the rag with the identical scent. You can use the command "Search." It goes without saying that you let it do its own searching and do not "help" it! Your dog has to do this all by itself. You should praise it enthusiastically when it has found the right rag.

## The more serious work

Being active together is lots of fun and no club or course is necessary to interact in a good way with your dog. However, you can learn a lot by participating in courses

*Searching*

*Start early with a hunting course to avoid mistakes in training*

and training. You get to know new people and, because training courses are given at a specific time, they foster some regularity. If you wish to take hunting courses with your dog or participate in a branch of dog sports such as agility or obedience, do not teach your dog any commands by yourself. The commands used in the training course can be fundamentally different from those you have taught your dog, and the exercises may also be performed somewhat differently. There is a good chance that

"mistakes" will be made that will have to be corrected later, which will take a lot of time and effort that you could otherwise have spared yourself and your dog.

*Sticks can be dangerous because they splinter*

# 13 DISEASES AND DEFECTS

*J.W.H.M. Strikkers, veterinary surgeon*

## How do you know when your dog is sick?

In order to tell whether an animal has a disease, it is important to be familiar with its normal behavior. How is its appetite, the amount it drinks, its urination, and its behavior in general? In the event of a difference in its usual behavior, it is important to take the dog's temperature (rectally). A dog's normal body temperature when at rest is between 99.5 and 101.3 degrees Fahrenheit (37.5 and 38.5 degrees Celsius). If the temperature is too high or too low, the dog has serious diarrhea or vomits frequently, it is necessary to contact your veterinarian.

*Taking its temperature*

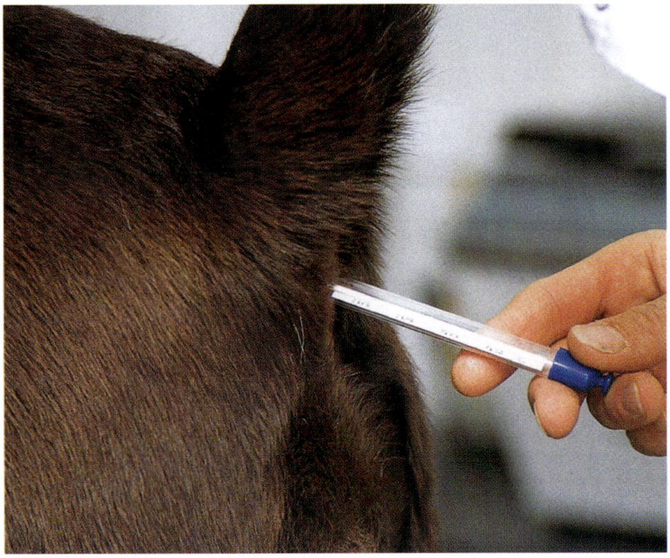

*Right: Enjoying the sun*

*Uteritis affects mostly older bitches*

## Uteritis

Uteritis is a common problem in bitches of four years and older, regardless of the breed. The ailment usually occurs four to eight weeks after heat or an anti-heat injection. The symptoms are usually listlessness, extra thirst, and sometimes a foul discharge from the vulva. Treatment with antibiotics of uteritis occurring four to eight weeks after heat usually has no effect. Not only is there a bacterial infection, but the uterine walls have usually degenerated as well. The only correct therapy is a hysterectomy. If action is taken too late, uteritis will be fatal.

## Prepuce infection

Prepuce infection is a common but not dangerous disorder which is not specific to Labrador Retrievers. The disorder can be recognized by the greenish discharge from the prepuce. Daily rinsing of the prepuce with a medicinal liquid, together with an ointment and/or pills, will promptly cure this infection. In 95 percent of the cases, castration is the only permanent solution to this problem.

## Poisoning

A dog that has been poisoned can show different symptoms, depending on the poison. These symptoms include vomiting, heavy drooling, diarrhea, stomach cramps, or chills. The dog sometimes has bald spots on the skin or goes into a coma. In order to save a dog that has been poisoned, it is not only important to consult a veterinarian as quickly as possible, but also to find out what kind of poison the animal has ingested. If possible, take the packaging with you to the vet. Some poisons must be vomited out, while that is precisely the wrong thing to do with others, such as paint thinner and gasoline. You would then do better to give your Labrador milk or raw eggs to prevent the poisonous substances from being absorbed by the body.

## Impacted anal glands

A dog's anal glands are to the left and right of its anus, about half an inch (one centimeter) inside. If your dog has problems with these glands, it will try to bite those places or to relieve the itch by dragging its hindquarters over the ground. A veterinarian can empty the anal glands, which gives

*The way the dog walks or lies does not always reveal everything about the quality of the hips*

immediate relief. If the problem occurs repeatedly, it is advisable to have the anal gland surgically removed.

## Hip dysplasia

Hip dysplasia (H.D.) is a common disorder, especially in larger breeds of dogs. H.D. is a generic name for development disorders in the coxo-femoral joint, which are determined by both hereditary and environmental factors. Dogs suffering from H.D. undergo an irreversible and steadily worse-

ning change in the hip joints. This change is characterized by a weakening of the synovial capsule, and swelling, weakening, and tearing of parts of the ligaments. The head of the femur and hip socket also develop abnormally. The joint cartilage is also affected, resulting in arthrosis. Dogs affected by this disorder have difficulty in standing up and/or walking, have less endurance, and sometimes develop a unilateral, alternating paralysis. Stretching the hips can be very painful. There is no real treatment for H.D., and a complete cure is therefore impossible. Through proper nutrition, good muscle training that is not too taxing for the dog, frequent movements in a straight line, and by guarding against overweight, the extent of the dog's problems with H.D. can be reduced. You can only know if your dog actually has H.D. after it has been officially X-rayed. No one can tell by the way it walks or lies; at most, it can only be suspected. Some dogs have severe H.D. without anyone ever noticing this, while others have a milder case and are seriously hindered by it. If the diagnosis of H.D. is made at an early age, surgical tilting of the pelvis gives a good prognosis. The pelvis is tilted over the hip socket, so that the hip joint can function normally without excessive wear and tear on the hip joint. This operation is, however, expensive, and is only performed in specialized animal clinics.
The dog can also be treated with painkillers, muscle strengthening medicines, and measured exercise. Homeopathic treatment or acupuncture can also give relief in some cases. An attempt is being made to combat this disease by breeding animals which have been officially tested and certified free of H.D.

***Elbow dysplasia is partly hereditary***

## Elbow dysplasia

Elbow dysplasia (E.D.) is a generic name for a group of elbow disorders which all have more or less the same cause, namely an unbalanced growth of the radius and ulna and/or developmental disorders in the bones surrounding the elbow joint. This may be due to a tendency inherited by the animal, but can also be influenced by environmental factors (food, exercise, and weight). E.D. includes L.P.A. (loose processus anconeus) and L.P.C.

*An Elizabethan collar prevents your dog from biting its wounds or stitches*

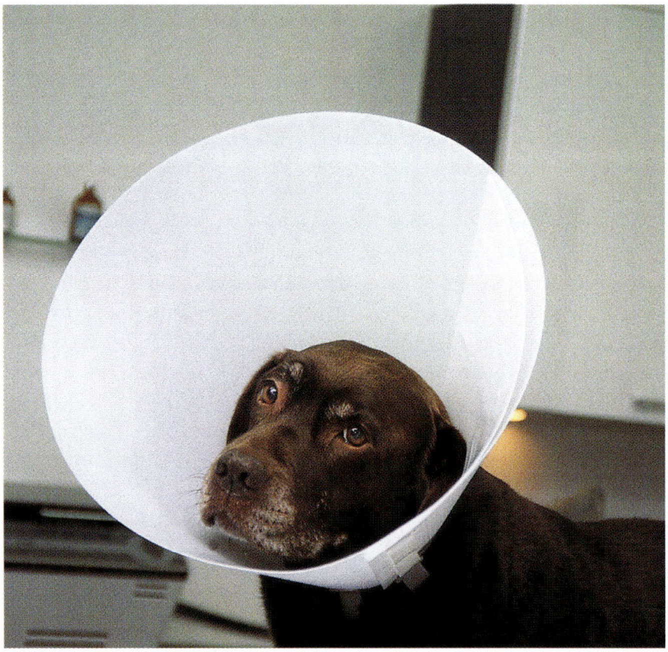

(loose processus coronoidus). Both problems involve a loose fragment of the ulna. The different names indicate the exact location of the problem. Another known problem is O.C.D. (osteochondrosis dissecans), which refers to a loose piece of cartilage of the humerus. "Incongruity of the elbow joint" refers to a poor connection of the elbow joint. Labrador Retrievers are mainly susceptible to L.P.C, O.C.D., and incongruity of the elbow joint. The symptoms of all three disorders are fairly similar. One or both forelegs is/are crippled, they have difficulty in standing up, and do not want to walk much or at all. Stretching the elbow joints is painful, and the elbows can be too full. Making a correct diagnosis is very important in view of the treatment. This can consist of surgically removing the loose fragment in the elbow joint, surgical correction of the length of the ulna, or rest with the appropriate anti-infection medicines. The sooner the diagnosis is made, the better the prognosis for the dog.
An attempt is being made to combat these disorders in Labrador Retrievers by X-raying prospective breeding animals and excluding affected animals from breeding.

## Progressive Retinal Atrophy

Progressive Retinal Atrophy (P.R.A.) is a disorder of the retina. In Labrador Retrievers from three to five years old,

*Only let your dog swim in safe waters*

the number of retinal cones is reduced, resulting in night blindness. If the deterioration of the retina continues, the rods can also be affected and the dog could become totally blind at five to nine years of age. It not possible to treat this disorder. This is a hereditary disease, and animals suffering from it should not be bred. Therefore, breeding animals are tested for this disease every year.

*This dog is suffering from an allergy*

*Your dog can get very sick from swallowing pieces of toys*

## Food allergies

A dog with a food allergy generally itches very badly all over its body and sometimes has a pimply rash in its groin, axillae, and on the stomach. Sometimes, there are also alternately soft and hard feces. Food allergies are caused by certain ingredients in the food. These can be chemical preservatives or coloring, but also certain proteins, such as beef, pork, or fish protein, that cause allergic reactions. In the first-mentioned case, the dog can be given food that does not contain any chemical ingredients. Lamb protein causes very few allergic reactions in dogs. If your dog is allergic to certain proteins, it is often sufficient to give food of which the protein is only lamb protein. Do not feed your dog anything else, in order to rule out the absorption of allergenic proteins.

## Atopy

Atopy is caused by an allergic reaction of the body to substances (allergens) breathed in. The external symptoms shown by your dog, such as biting and licking its feet, dragging its head

over the floor, and scratching its axillae and groin, are caused by the reactions to these allergens. Allergens include dust mites tree and grass pollen, and also cats, dogs, and human skin particles. The first signs of atopy appear between six months and three years of age. An allergy test will show which allergens cause the strongest reaction in your dog. The most effective treatment of atopy is to ensure the least possible contact between your dog and the allergens. This is often not feasible in practice, for example, if your dog is allergic to flakes of human skin. Nevertheless, it is very important to minimize contact. In the event of a dust mite allergy, this will mean that you have to vacuum frequently and replace soft floor coverings with wood, laminate, or tiles.
Good grooming of the coat is also important. Regular combing or brushing is a real necessity. The dog may also be bathed with a mild, medicinal shampoo. Good nutrition is also of essential importance. The food must contain sufficient nutrients for the skin and coat. The addition of special fatty acids by mixing a dermatological oil with the food can also improve the situation.

## Hot spots

Hot spots occur when the dog bites into its skin in several places. Hot spots are common in Labradors, but also in Golden Retrievers. They can be caused by a flea bite, but also a slight

*Balls are fine toys, but ones that are too small or too soft can be dangerous*

irritation as a result of shedding. The dog will scratch and lick itself thus causing the coat to become wet, which results in an infection of the underlying skin. This causes additional irritation and perpetuates the cycle.
Treatment consists of cleansing the spots twice a day with betadine shampoo in combination with an antibacterial ointment.

## Other causes of itch

Not only atopy, hot spot, and food allergy can cause itch and other problems in dogs. Dogs can also have allergic reactions to flea saliva. One single bite is then sufficient to cause an

*If your dog is listless, it could be sick*

allergic reaction. Mites can also cause problems. Mites cannot be seen with the naked eye, but your veterinarian has special equipment to determine whether or not these parasites are present and to start treatment.

# 14 Breeding

## A litter: fun?

You have a bitch and would like her to have a litter. Although a litter of Labradors can be great fun, it is not good to romanticize this event too much. You are taking on a serious responsibility. Do you remember how high your expectations were on the day you went to pick up your puppy at the breeder's? You

*A good breeding bitch is not only beautiful, but also very healthy, and has a good character*

expected a mentally and physically healthy, friendly, well imprinted, and also beautiful puppy, and hopefully you were not disappointed. The people taking home a puppy from your bitch will have the same expectations. You owe it to them, as well as to the "new" puppies, to take a critical look not just at the characteristics of your bitch and the sire, but also your family situation.

*Right: You can see many males together at shows*

### Look before you leap

Never breed a litter because you think it will make your bitch more gentle or beautiful. If your bitch is not already gentle, she is not suitable as a breeding bitch. A bitch seldom becomes more beautiful after having carried, whelped, and suck-

3554

led a large litter. The milk glands of most bitches will never regain their original form, and motherhood will always be visible. Nor should you breed a litter because you think it will make you rich, because that will not happen. The whole process prior to the service, but also the service itself, the birth, and the raising of the pups can be fraught with complications requiring professional assistance, including expensive veterinary treatment. Even if all goes well, you would definitely need a financial buffer for, among other things, the (paid) services of the sire, food, pedigree application, vaccinations, and tests. In addition, you must definitely have the right attitude. Not everyone has the capacity to care for and assist the bitch and her puppies. This takes a lot of time, effort, and dedication, month after month, day in and day out. When your bitch has puppies, you cannot leave her alone for a single day. Labradors can have large litters. On average, you can expect six to eight puppies, but a litter of twelve puppies is among the possibilities. Puppies produce feces and urine, and the surroundings of the litter must therefore be thoroughly cleaned and disinfected several times a day. In their rumbunctious moments, the puppies can make a lot of noise that can cause problems with the neighbors. You also need to imprint and socialize the puppies properly.
This will continue afterward as well. New owners can sometimes call you years later with questions about their dog and, in order to answer them, you need to have more than a general knowledge of dogs, in particular Labrador Retrievers. That is another task you take upon yourself when considering a litter.

## The bitch

A suitable breeding bitch has a character that is friendly, stable, and typical of the breed. Her willingness to work has been proven in field-trials. She is in excellent condition and naturally she is a beautiful representative of her breed; not just in your eyes, but also in those of one or more inspectors who have judged her positively at shows. Her hips as well as her elbows have been certified. Hip and elbow dysplasia are (partly) hereditary disorders that occur in the breed. No one can tell by looking at her whether she is free of these disorders. This can only be determined by an official X-ray, which is assessed by a committee of specialists. The same applies to her eyes, because several hereditary eye disorders are also known to occur in the breed. Consider that your bitch can pass on more to her puppies than is immediately apparent. In her genes, she carries the characteristics of her parents and ancestors, which can reappear in the litter. Research of her pedigree is thus to be recommended.

## The sire of the puppies

Suitable sires for your bitch can be found at shows, via the breed club, and in club magazines. The male should have at least the same, but preferably better, qualities than your bitch. Just like your bitch, a male must also have healthy, stable dogs as parents and ancestors. If the male's owner has the best interests of the breed at heart, then you will also have to submit the pedigree, show, and test results of your bitch. Even if both dogs are good representatives of their breed, however, this does not automatically mean that the combination will be good. If you have good contact with the breeder of your dog, ask their opinion and also that of the sire's owner.

## Deviating coat colors

Three colors of Labrador Retrievers are recognized: black, yellow, and brown. The brown color can vary from the light milk chocolate which is less appreciated at shows to the highly praised dark brown coat color. In addition, we occasionally see "yellow-livers," dogs with a yellow coat, but with liver

***Black, yellow, and brown***

pigmentation on its nose, lips, and eye rims. These "yellow-livers" are not desired at shows because of the absence of black pigment, but can be used for breeding if they have other valuable qualities. This is also true for several other color deviations, such as yellow dogs with black spots or dogs with white spots in other places than the breast, such as the head or neck. There are several other deviating coat colors, which cannot all be discussed here. What you must take into consideration in any case is that there is always a chance of one or more "wrong colored" puppies in a litter. These are pups that cannot be shown, but they do not differ in any other way from their littermates. You need to find loving owners for such puppies, who have no interest in shows. The chance of "yellow-livers" and other pigmentation and coat color deviations can be reduced considerably or even exclu-

*Two different tones of brown; the darker one is the favorite at shows*

ded if you inform yourself well about the possible hereditary color and pigmentation genes of your bitch and the chosen sire, and what possible pigmentation and coat color can be expected from this combination. Experienced breeders can tell you more about this on the basis of your bitch's pedigree, but you can also contact the Labrador club.

## The service

A bitch is usually serviced first during her third or fourth heat. An earlier time is not recommended, because a bitch is usually not emotionally stable enough, nor sufficiently full-grown physically. Later in life, fertility is usually reduced and the chance of complications is greater. Long before the service, you will have had your bitch wormed; she should also have had her vaccinations in good time. Furthermore, she will be free of parasites and must certainly not be too fat. You can expect your bitch to be in heat twice a year. It can be recognized from the swelling of the vulva and some loss of blood. Most bitches are fertile between the tenth and thirteenth day of estrus and will allow service during that time. To increase the chance of success, it is customary, after one day's rest in between, to have the bitch serviced again. After service, the penis of the male swells up, through which process the animals remain attached by their sex organs. This "coupling" can last anything from ten minutes to three quarters of an hour. Sometimes, however, coupling does not take place at all; this has no effect on the successful fertilization of the bitch.

## The gestation period

The average gestation period of a bitch is nine weeks, counting from the day of the first service. In the first four weeks of the period, you do not have to make any special provisions, but it goes without saying that you should not bother her too much during the entire gestation period. Take her for a quiet walk several times a day to prevent her from getting out of condition. Do not give her any extra vitamins or medicines without your veterinarian's advice, because they could affect the development of the embryos. If you want to use an anti-flea remedy, you should also first consult your vet.
From about the fifth week on, the line of your bitch's stomach will change and her milk glands will swell somewhat. If you want to know earlier if your bitch is pregnant, you can have her examined on the twenty-eighth day by a vet. It has been discovered that on that day the embryos can best be felt and seen by echography.

*Pregnant bitches need more food*

Your bitch will not need extra food until the fifth week. Because the pups take up more and more room, your bitch can no longer digest large quantities of food. It is better to give her smaller portions throughout the day. Her daily rations can gradually be doubled and then cut back around the time the puppies begin to eat by themselves.

## Whelping

**The whelping box**
Whelping can best take place in a whelping box made especially for this purpose. The whelping box functions for weeks afterward as a nest for the dam and puppies. The material must therefore be sturdy and easy to disinfect. In connection with

rising cold, to which both dam and puppies are very sensitive, the whelping box should never stand directly on the floor, but always on a pallet. Do not use newspapers in the whelping box, but thin, corrugated cardboard. This material is a good support for the puppies and does not leak any ink. You can introduce your bitch to the whelping box during the seventh week of gestation.

| |
|---|
| The ideal size for a whelping box is: 40 in. long x 50 in. wide x 20 in. high (100 cm long x 125 cm wide x 50 cm high) |

**Supplies**
Long before the whelping, you should have the following supplies available:

- digital thermometer
- stacks of clean towels
- a thick role of corrugated cardboard
- puppy bottle and nipples
- a good substitute bitch milk
- disinfectant
- accurate kitchen scale
- red heating lamp (incubator lamp)

**The home stretch**
Even though your bitch normally appreciates your company and that of others, in the first few weeks she is more in need of rest. Regulated by hormones, she can become nervous from too much attention to her and her puppies, and start dragging her young elsewhere. Therefore, place the whelping box in a quiet place. Each whelping is different, and complications are always possible. Good contact with the breeder of your bitch, the owner

***Pregnant bitch***

of the sire, or the veterinarian is invaluable, so that in these days of uncertainty you will have some support, possibly by telephone. Find out whether your vet is prepared to come in the evening, weekend, or middle of the night if necessary. Not every vet is enthusiastic about this. If you are uncertain about your capacities for maternity assistance, ask an experienced person to help you.
Although the average gestation period is 63 days, your bitch may decide to bring her litter into the world a few days earlier or later. The date you have circled on your calendar is therefore only a guide.
The body temperature of most bitches drops a little 24 hours before whelping. You can check this by taking her temperature (rectally) every day at the same time.
A few days before whelping, many bitches become restless. The nesting urge is often expressed by digging and scratching in the whelping box, but also by digging holes in the garden. Do not let your bitch go outside by herself in the last few days, especially if she digs holes. Bitches sometimes decide to give birth outside, in a sometimes cold, damp, and not at all sterile environment.

**Birth**

The birth begins when your bitch begins to have her first contractions. These contractions can easily be distinguished from other labor, because the flanks press strongly together. The

***Puppies less than one week old***

first puppy is usually born an hour after the first contraction. The puppy is often still wrapped in its membrane and connected by the umbilical cord to the placenta, which follows either immediately or later. Always note the passing of a placenta; if one or more remain in the womb, this could result in a life-threatening infection.

The bitch will bite through the membrane and the umbilical cord and lick the puppy clean and dry. If your bitch is a bit clumsy or you have the idea that she does not understand what

to do, then you will have to cut the umbilical cord yourself, remove the membrane, and rub the puppies dry. Most importantly, however, you will have to remove the surrounding membrane and if necessary the mucus and fluid from the mouth and nose, so that the puppies can breathe.
Generally speaking, the bitch will eat the placentas, and you can simply allow her to do so. If she has more than five puppies, it is better to remove the rest of the placentas. The next pup may follow immediately after the first, but it could also come half an hour or even more than an hour later. If you suspect that something is wrong, contact your vet.
Once the entire litter has been born, the bitch will calm down. Give her some water to drink and take her into the garden so that she can do her business. Someone else can use that time to clean and disinfect the whelping box.

## The puppies

### Marking and weighing

*To be able to follow their individual growth and development properly, you need to mark the puppies*

If you have several puppies of the same color and the same sex, you need to mark them, otherwise you will not be able to keep track of their individual growth and development. You can mark them with nail polish, for example on their toes or back. Weigh each puppy, note the weight at birth, special characteristics, sex, and time of birth. The average birth weight of Labradors is about 14 ounces (400 grams). You should then weigh the puppies every day at the same time and note down your findings in a schedule. This will make it easier to detect any growth stagnation or defects.

### Aftercare

After the whelping is over, ask your veterinarian to come by and examine the puppies and bitch. Most vets will give an injection to help the uterus contract. Any (pieces of) placenta or even puppies left behind can then be passed and will not be able to cause problems. Ask your vet for a wormer for the puppies and keep precisely to the worming schedule. All puppies have worms, even if the dam has been wormed regularly.

*Labrador Retrievers usually have large litters*

### The first weeks after birth

Keep a close eye on your bitch during the first few weeks. Take her temperature every day and be on the alert for sudden rises and drops. Also keep an eye on the milk glands, which should not change color or become hard. The puppies have sharp nails and the bitch will certainly appreciate it if you clip or file them. Discharge from the vulva, first red then fading to light pink, is not alarming but very natural. A heat lamp will not be needed in the summer, but in other cases it will be necessary to maintain the right temperature for the puppies. Hang it above the whelping box about 8 inches. (20 cm) above the shoulder height of your bitch. The first week of a puppy's life consists of drinking and sleeping. As long as the puppies are not fed anything additional, the bitch will massage their stomachs to encourage excrement, which she then cleans up neatly.
If your bitch has sufficient milk and takes good care of her puppies, you will hardly ever hear them whine. If the puppies

*At this age, the puppies are well aware of what goes on around them*

crawl about whining pitifully, this could indicate a shortage of food or a different problem. In such a case, contact your veterinarian.
About the tenth day, the eyes open, and at the age of two or three weeks the pups take their first uncertain and wobbly steps in the whelping box.

**Imprinting**
Until puppies have been vaccinated, they are very susceptible to disease. Although they receive antibodies from the mother's milk, these do not protect them against everything. Germs are brought in by other dogs, but also on the soles of your shoes or outer clothing. Therefore, have everyone who comes to look at the puppies take their shoes off and disinfect their hands, and keep visits from strangers to a minimum during the first few weeks. Keep your suckling bitch off the street and only let

***Between the third and fourth week after birth, the pups can learn to eat by themselves***

her out in your own garden. However, the puppies should not be kept too far removed from everyday life, since it is necessary for them to get acquainted with the things that are so commonplace to us. Allow them to be picked up and cuddled by a calm child under supervision and feel free to turn on the television or radio. These small things can make a world of difference in their later character development.

**The fourth to sixth week**
Depending on the size of the litter and the condition of the bitch, you can start giving the puppies additional food when they are three to five weeks old. Buy special puppy food at your pet shop. Not all pet shops have this food in stock, so it is better to order it in advance. Some breeders prefer to use human baby food, but puppy weaning food is more suited to the nutritional requirements of puppies.
Once the puppies have become accustomed to puppy weaning food, you can gradually get them used to dry puppy food. In the

*A group of young Labradors playing their favorite game: making a mess*

beginning, you can soak it in warm water, so that it softens. Cooked and puréed red meat and cooked chicken can be given without any problem. Always disinfect the dishes or bowls from which the puppies eat and drink after use. This is certainly necessary in the summer months. As soon as the puppies start to eat by themselves, the bitch considers her work to be done and no longer cleans up the urine and feces of her young. From then on, you will have to do this several times a day. It goes without saying that you should do this very thoroughly, and also disinfect the whelping box and surrounding area every day.

**On their own feet**

When the puppies are about six or seven weeks old, most bitches begin to withdraw a little from them. Many bitches appreciate it enormously if they do not have to stay with them all the time and are taken with you for a walk. Puppies of this age are very lively and play a lot, for which they need room. A litter of puppies is easier to raise in the spring and summer than during the wet and cold winter months.

Around this period or as soon as the puppies have virtually ceased to drink from their mother, it is time for their first vaccinations. At the age of eight to ten weeks, they can go to their new owners.

*The activities of pups barely a week old consist of drinking and sleeping*

# USEFUL ADDRESSES

The Labrador Retriever Club, Inc.
14686 Grand Army of the Republic Highway
Hambden, Ohio 44024
www.thelabradorclub.com

Canadian Kennel Club/Club Canin Canadien
89 Skyway Avenue, Suite 100
Etobicoke, Ontario
M9W 6R4
www.ckc.ca

# ACKNOWLEDGMENTS AND PHOTO CREDITS

All photographs were taken by Esther Verhoef.
The black-and-white illustration is taken from the book Hondenrassen by Count Van Bylandt.

The author and the publisher wish to thank all persons and bodies that have cooperated in the photography for this book, but especially B. and J. van den Bergh, A. Roefs, and J. van Gils, on whose premises most of the dogs in the pictures were photographed, and Van Riel Distripet in Waalwijk and Dynabone in Kruisland, for making available the photographs of some of the products illustrated.